Conversations in Garden History

New Research
New Ideas
New Approaches

Editor
Pippa Potts

History of Gardens and Designed Landscapes Seminar
Institute of Historical Research

INSTITUTE OF HISTORICAL RESEARCH | University of London School of Advanced Study

Birkbeck Garden History Group

BGHG

Contact: lhrgardenhistory@gmail.com

First Edition
ISBN: 978-0-9554414-3-1

Cover image: Detail of Anon, *Frontispice: épidémie de peste à Florence (1348) et entretien des conteurs du Décameron,* c. 1465-1470, Bibliothèque nationale de France, MS Fr 129, f.1; Wikimedia Commons

Published by
Birkbeck Garden History Group

Project Editor
Susan Jellis

The **Birkbeck Garden History Group (BGHG)** was founded in 2002 by students of the Birkbeck College's Garden History courses which began in 1995. It now has members with a variety of study backgrounds. BGHG organises lectures and study days on garden history topics, visits to gardens of historical interest, and occasional gallery tours or library visits and private views of garden history relevance. Members receive a newsletter three times a year. BGHG supports garden history education through occasional small grants and has also previously published three collections of postgraduate research papers in garden history: *Grand Gardens and Green Spaces* (2006); *Fantasy, Form and Function* (2010); and *Digging Deeper* (2019).

Email: bghginfo@gmail.com
https://birkbeckgardenhistory.org.uk

CONTENTS

FOREWORD

It is a real pleasure to introduce this new collection of research papers on the history of gardens and landscapes. The papers emerge from the History of Gardens and Landscapes Seminar which has been part of the Institute of Historical Research seminar community for two decades now, with backing from its own Supporters' Group, the Birkbeck Garden History Group, and the Gardens Trust. It is particularly apt that this book should emerge in the Seminar's twentieth anniversary year: 2023

The History of Gardens and Landscapes Seminar is one of the many research seminars that sit at the heart of intellectual life at the Institute of Historical Research. Some of these emerged before the Second World War, others as recently as 2021. Each Seminar has a distinctive character, and has developed in ways that reflect and support the working practices of particular specialisms, spinning around shared intellectual interests and common research questions. Each seminar community mobilises its members to present, to listen, and crucially, to discuss. Dialogue sits at the heart of the seminar model, reflecting the way collaboration is baked into all types of history-making, and demonstrating the benefits of bringing together expertise in pursuit of new knowledge and understanding. Whilst the difficulties of recent times have shaped the mechanisms through which the IHR seminars meet, the possibilities offered by the online and hybrid form have allowed the seminars to extend their communities both nationally and internationally.

The Seminar that has provided such rich inspiration for the chapters presented here draws its speakers from across the United Kingdom and beyond. The 2022-23 programme has, for example, showcased work from scholars based in Mississippi, Mexico, New York, London, Florence, York and St Andrews. The Seminar has also long been committed to bringing together all those who work with gardens and landscapes history and who are interested in it. The specialist community includes historians to be sure, but also architects, gardeners, horticulturalists, planners, geographers, artists and photographers. The Seminar transcends disciplinary and professional distinctions creating a productive interdisciplinary and cross-sector space where new ideas and approaches can be tested and developed.

The title of this collection – *Conversations in Garden History* – speaks to its roots in the seminar context. The papers presented here reflect the intellectual openness of the seminar as well as its temporal and geographical range. Readers will move from beekeeping in seventeenth century England to Singapore's garden city in the second half of the twentieth century, visiting Detroit, Aranjuez and Aztec Mexico along the way. The diversity of topic and approach is testament to the power of collaboration and the importance of thinking and talking together about the past.

Professor Claire Langhamer
Director
Institute of Historical Research

INTRODUCTION

CHRISTINE LALUMIA

Facilitating conversation and making connections have long been core aims of the History of Gardens and Landscapes Seminar at the Institute of Historical Research. The conversation begins when often unpublished research is presented by an invited speaker to a meeting of the Seminar. The convenors have always sought to bring new ideas arising from current academic work and professional practice to the fore, making every effort to make connections between differing but related disciplines, which all look to gardens, landscapes and their histories as a key focus or inspiration.

For more than ten years it has been the Seminar's practice to build termly programmes around a central theme. The chapter titles in this book are in fact those of themes pursued during the past five years (see page 136) and although the essays in each chapter are not necessarily based on papers presented in the eponymous programme, they are still the work of speakers who have participated in the Seminar. Some contributors will be familiar names but others may be new to readers, individuals who are not yet well known in mainstream garden history circles but deserve to be. They hail from different backgrounds – both academic and geographical – and bring to garden history an impressive body of experience and knowledge, individually and collectively.

We have envisioned this publication as sharing some of the spirit of convivial dialogue and exploration that we see in the cover's depiction of men and women in Giovanni Boccaccio's *The Decameron* conversing in a garden. Like the protagonists in that book, the contributors included in this publication weave stories, themes and ideas in compelling and original ways. Each chapter is a dialogue, presenting two different approaches to the same subject. However, the conversations are not limited to the chapters they start in, but link with others throughout the book. Thus, for example, and most explicitly related to storytelling like *The Decameron,* are the papers written by Katherine Myers and Jason Allen-Paisant. Myers engages through close reading of the text and Allen-Paisant through conversations with two wise but very different people: his own grandmother and a Rasta herbalist. Central to both is the language of plants and the intimate and deep understanding of plants and their meanings, which can be seen in seventeenth-century England and as strongly in contemporary Jamaica.

Money, Money, Money was a theme which attracted some very stimulating papers and speakers. While it had a tongue-in-cheek reference to pop music, it was, more seriously, a reminder that money, commerce, trade and speculation are often inseparable from garden making. The first chapter in this volume takes up the theme with a reprinting of a paper which was published in *Historical Research* after its author, Keith Alcorn, was put forward for the IHR's Pollard Prize for a paper given to the History of Gardens and Landscapes Seminar. Alcorn uses his interest in economic history to analyse London's nursery trade and the vogue for 'exotic' plants in the nineteenth century. Francesca Murray's paper on mutual aid societies explores the support given to those involved in professional horticulture, providing an opportunity to see nineteenth-century garden history through an altogether different prism.

The global pandemic was the initial spur for the *Greening Responses to Crisis and Catastrophe* programme, but issues such as climate change and related environmental issues, combined with widespread worries about the flora and fauna of our planet reinforced the decision to adopt this theme. In the relevant chapter in this volume, and taking the examples of Singapore and Detroit respectively, Jesse O'Neill and Michael Ann Mullen provide illuminating insights into the very different ways in which urban greening has, and is, changing both the appearance and conception of what urban spaces can be. The links between O'Neill and Mullen's two very different stories of urban transformation, both of which are laden with political and commercial concerns, make a fascinating 'conversation'.

The theme of *Gardens, Politics and Power* featured much new and original research and reminded us of what fertile ground this is for future garden history research. Drawn from the programme are the two papers in the chapter of the same name. Margaret Goehring's insightful discussion of the gardens of sixteenth-century Aranjuez in Spain grew out of her deep knowledge of Medieval and Renaissance manuscripts and shows how the concept of the 'Burgundian Garden', in its many facets, was used to express power both in northern Europe and in Spain. Jeanne Gillespie's work focuses on a slightly earlier period in the 'new world' where beautiful cities and gardens were just as important as a political tool as they were in Spain, albeit achieved through an onerous system of tribute. The ingenuity of the Mexica people in responding to the tribute demanded of them finds its echo both in the work of many diverse groups and individuals in Detroit and in the tenacity of Jamaicans growing crops in inhospitable sites on the island or in Britain as described by Allen-Paisant in *Conversations across Continents.*

In the same chapter, *Conversations across Continents,* Alan Starr traces connections between an English estate and the investments in Jamaica which funded its beautification. Starr's piece could, arguably, have been included here under the heading of *Money Money Money*. It reminds us that Britain's colonial past and the ways in which it relates to gardens and the funding of garden making in the West is topical, a subject which must be better examined and understood and on which there is currently much work being done. As with Starr, so Marlis Hinckley's study of political life seen through the lens of the complex life of bees, which is part of the conversation in *New Perspectives on the Seventeenth Century*, might well have been included in *Gardens, Politics and Power.* The same observation about the interchangeability of subjects can be made about several other contributions to the book, underlining the fluid nature – and strength – of garden and landscape history.

The final papers in this volume is the work of a poet and writer, which again signals the strength of interest in garden and landscape history and highlights how much excellent, original work on gardens and designed landscapes is being done across disciplines around the world, something it is perhaps easy to lose sight of when considering the decline in the number of formal degree courses in garden history on offer in Britain. Designed to celebrate the vibrancy of the discipline, and the twentieth anniversary of the History of Gardens and Landscapes Seminar in a tangible way, we hope this publication will give further impetus to conversations that help clarify ideas, encourage debate and stimulate ever more excitement about garden history.

1

MONEY, MONEY, MONEY

The conversation in this chapter juxtaposes two very different aspects of the economics of the gardening business in nineteenth-century Britain. Put very starkly, a flourishing nursery business is set against the threat of the workhouse for the gardener.

It is well known that the nineteenth century saw a boom in gardening activity thanks to a sustained period of economic growth, wealth accumulation, technological innovation and greatly improved communications. Here the picture is given greater depth by new research into how, in the first half of the century, the London nursery trade responded, and even contributed, to the boom, providing exotics for both the aristocracy and gentry on one hand and the emerging middle class on the other. As England's most important port, London had a long history as a place where exotic plants were collected and cultivated, but the start of a truly commercial nursery trade dates to the mid-seventeenth century, with men like George London and Henry Wise leading the way from their Brompton Park nursery. A close examination of the records of these men's nineteenth-century successors demonstrates an ability not just to breed and trade in exotics but also to adopt new business practices.

The growth of gardening in the nineteenth century inevitably meant a rise in the number of people engaged in the activity. Some were the amateurs who bought plants from the nurseries and were prepared to get their own hands dirty in what was increasingly seen as a respectable and healthy leisure pursuit. But there were also those who depended on gardening for a living, many of whom were drawn to the rapidly expanding towns and cities. The story of the nineteenth-century gardener is generally under-researched but this section of the chapter addresses one particular aspect, that of the provision of financial support in times of need for a relatively poorly paid group of men. The proliferation of friendly societies and mutual aid associations was the background to the creation of the Gardeners' Royal Benevolent Institution (GBI) in 1839. This organization was important, it is argued here, not only as a potential lifeline but also for bringing people employed in disparate branches of horticulture together in an unprecedented fashion.

FROM SPECIMENS TO COMMODITIES: THE LONDON NURSERY TRADE AND THE INTRODUCTION OF EXOTIC PLANTS IN THE EARLY-NINETEENTH CENTURY

KEITH ALCORN

ABSTRACT

Nursery owners played a critical role in transforming imported plants and trees from scientific specimens into commodities that became widespread in British gardens in the first half of the nineteenth century. This paper uses rare surviving business records of London nurserymen to investigate the scale and structure of the nursery trade and its business practices between 1800 and 1850 and how nursery businesses innovated to meet the needs of an emerging middle class.*

INTRODUCTION

Writing to his son James in America in 1821, the journalist and politician William Cobbett held out the prospect of a new business venture that would provide his son with a good living. A nursery business selling trees and shrubs grown from seeds gathered in America would do very well, Cobbett thought, and 'it gives me great pleasure to introduce and spread things of this sort'.[1] James Cobbett and George Woodcock of New York were charged with gathering vast quantities of American tree seed to be shipped to England, and for several years Cobbett sent Woodcock detailed lists of the seeds he required, the best locations to gather the seed and the right times to visit these locations.[2] The black locust tree (*Robinia pseudoacacia)* with its beautiful wisteria-like white blossoms, the tulip tree (*Liriodendron tulipifera)* with its orange flowers and buttery autumn colour, the black walnut (*Juglans nigra*) and *Magnolia glauca*, 'the finest shrub in the world ... above all things let me have a lot of these', were among the trees propagated from imported seed at Cobbett's nursery in Kensington and gradually spread through the British Isles.[3] They still adorn London streets and British gardens today but their exotic origins are rarely discerned by those who enjoy their colour and variety. American trees formed the first wave of the exotic plants from Britain's colonies (and former colonies) that were to transform Britain's landscapes and gardens in the nineteenth century. Within a few years of its establishment William and James Cobbett's seed farm and nursery at Kensington was a thriving business, assisted perhaps by the connections that Cobbett would have established when he was employed as a gardener in the Royal Botanic Gardens at Kew in his youth.[4]

**This paper is an edited and illustrated version of one first delivered to the IHR's History of Gardens and Landscapes Seminar. It was originally published in* Historical Research, *93 (2020), pp. 715-733,* https://doi.org/10.1093/hisres/htaa025. *I would like to thank Felix Driver, Zoe Laidlaw, the convenors of the IHR seminar and the anonymous reviewers for* Historical Research *for their help and advice. The research was funded by the Arts and Humanities Research Council [AH/L503940/1].*

Cobbett's decision to specialize in American trees and shrubs, exploiting his American connections, proved to be a shrewd business decision.[5] Writing in 1835, the impresario of horticultural publishing John Claudius Loudon observed that the nursery business had undergone a substantial transformation in the two preceding decades. Whereas nurseries in the vicinity of London and Edinburgh had dominated the supply of trees twenty years previously, by 1835 'all the forest trees, and the more common of the fruit trees, are procured by planters from nurseries in their immediate neighbourhood; and the demand on the metropolitan nurseries is limited to the less common articles, or to what is new'.[6] He went on to identify the chief vulnerabilities of the trade: the high rents charged for nursery ground in the vicinity of London and 'the very long credit generally taken by country gentlemen'. These factors, rather than high running costs, explained the high prices that nurseries were forced to charge for plants not commonly held by provincial nurseries.[7] Specialization was advantageous if a business could accumulate the expertise and connections to acquire and cultivate exotic imports (plants from outside Europe not already naturalized in the British Isles), and enabled nurseries to charge high prices for rarities. The structure of businesses themselves also dictated the direction of development and the abrupt disappearance of traders.

This paper examines how plants from Britain's expanding empire re-made the British garden during this period, looking at the relationship between nursery businesses, botanical gardens and the domestic garden. Plant introductions resulted from British engagement with non-native flora, whether as traders, colonizers, botanical explorers or plant collectors.[8] Nurseries participated in, and profited from, these processes of plant introduction, as well as supporting the development of botanical science through the provision of plants for illustration and dialogue with botanists over nomenclature and classification. Furthermore, as Sarah Easterby-Smith has demonstrated in the case of two businesses in London and Paris, nursery owners acted as important intermediaries between scientific networks and wider publics in the late eighteenth century.[9] Nurseries were also important partners of the Royal Botanic Gardens at Kew in plant collecting overseas, sponsoring expeditions and sharing their discoveries. But little is known about the day-to-day operations of the trade, its scale or the factors that led to the emergence of businesses that specialized in exotic plants or trees. Was there a specialist trade in exotic plants by the early nineteenth century that promoted their introduction and how was that trade structured? This paper examines the organization of the plant nursery trade – as distinct from the growth of fruit and vegetables in market gardening – during the early decades of the nineteenth century, the scale of business activity, and the increasing pressures on nursery businesses to specialize. In particular, it evaluates Loudon's claims regarding the effects of debt and specialization on nursery businesses using the only London nursery business records to have survived from the early nineteenth century: Colvill's Exotic Nursery, Samuel Harrison's Nursery, and James Cochran, a hybrid nursery and gardening business. (No business records exist for William Cobbett's nursery and seed business.) The paper analyses the management of debt by businesses in some detail, approaching the issue as a question of business practice rather than individual character, to provide insight into the way in which debt management operated in early nineteenth-century small businesses prior to the widespread utilization of bank lending and instruments of credit.[10] It concludes by examining how ways of doing business evolved up to 1840 as owners took advantage of new opportunities to expand their clientele and the ways in which nursery owners encouraged new forms of consumption among the aristocratic elite and the urban middle class.

THE EXTENT AND SCALE OF THE EARLY-NINETEENTH-CENTURY NURSERY TRADE IN LONDON

The role of the nursery trade in the creation of British gardens and landscapes has tended to be subordinated to writing the history of garden design and plant discovery.[11] Yet, as Kathleen Clark has demonstrated in respect of the early eighteenth century, without the nursery trade, the large-scale planting of the eighteenth-century landscape garden would not have been possible.[12] Nor would nineteenth-century gardens have acquired exotic plants so quickly, in such variety. Nurseries provided the means through which botanical specimens were transformed into commodities, and hence cultivated at the scale required to achieve transformations in the urban and rural landscape. Large nursery businesses already existed by the middle of the eighteenth century in London and the provinces and some carried large stocks of North American trees and shrubs. Specialization by nurseries was already apparent by the late seventeenth century and the use of catalogues to market plants was apparent by the mid eighteenth century.[13] This specialization intensified by the end of the century but, as this article will demonstrate, the early nineteenth century trade delivered innovations in discovery, scale, marketing and distribution techniques. These are discussed in the second part of the paper.[14]

In 1786 John Abercrombie published a list of fifty-eight nurseries within eight or ten miles of London, while Thomas Milne's maps of Middlesex drawn between 1795 and 1799 show forty-five nursery businesses (Figure 1).[15] By 1841 the Post Office London Directory listed at least 122 nursery businesses.[16] Judging by the names listed, this trade appears to have been male-dominated but more work is needed to understand the role of women as family members, proprietors and workers in these businesses.[17] Nurseries were particularly concentrated in the fertile flood plain to the west of London, on the King's Road, in Hammersmith and in Fulham. The concentration of nurseries in this district was partly a function of their proximity to highways leading to the suburbs of west London and the Thames Valley, which had become fashionable locations during the eighteenth century.[18] The concentration of fruit growing for the London market on the roads north of the Thames between Kensington and Twickenham may also have encouraged nursery businesses to congregate in this area.[19] (Market gardens were concentrated almost exclusively on the north side of the Thames from Fulham to Teddington, with the largest concentrations in Chiswick and Isleworth.) In 1818 there were ten nurseries or florists in the 275-yard stretch of road then known as King's Road, including Colvill's Exotic Nursery near Sloane Square, and Joseph Knight's Royal Exotic Nursery (later Knight & Perry) on the King's Road opposite what is now Lots Road.[20]

Another arc of nursery grounds could be found on the eastern fringes of the City of London, extending from Mile End through Hackney and the Kingsland Road to Clapton and the Lea Valley (which became a site of market gardening that persisted well into the twentieth century).[21] Thomson's and Gordon's Nursery in Mile End, Loddiges' Nursery in Hackney and Messrs. Low in Clapton were the most prominent dealers in exotic plants to the east of London.[22] In his 1798 survey of agriculture in Middlesex, John Middleton estimated that around 1,500 acres in the county were devoted to nursery grounds, producing around £100,000 a year in revenue.[23] Converting this sum to present-day value using the labour earnings index, nursery grounds generated around £123 million a year in today's money.[24] Subsequent conversions using labour value for commodities and labour earnings for revenue appear in brackets after the original sum.

Figure 1. Thomas Milne's Map of Middlesex, 1795-1799, British Library, Maps K.Top.6.95. Nurseries, coloured orange, and marked with an 'n'.[25]

In his 1839 guide to London nurseries James Mangles identified fourteen businesses in London and eight businesses in the south or west of England that specialized in varieties of exotic plants and were 'celebrated for particular classes of plants'.[26] Only two of the nurseries he recommended in London did not specialize in exotics, but outside London his list of 130 nursery and seed businesses includes only eight businesses where specific mention is made of exotic stock, and this list does not include Backhouse of York, Dickson of Edinburgh or Messrs. Veitch of Exeter, all known to be dealing in exotic plants by this time.[27] Analysing nursery catalogues up to 1837, John Harvey found that exotic plants tended to disseminate slowly from the capital to provincial nurseries, and that the London nurseries and seed companies appeared to predominate in the trade.[28] Loudon partly attributed the growing difficulties facing the nursery business in the 1830s to the wider dissemination of propagation techniques, which led to greater competition for specialists.[29] Caution should therefore be exercised when inferring from trade catalogues of the period that plants were less available outside London, or that there was little demand for plants which disappear from catalogues: Loudon noted that for many nurserymen, new plants remained profitable only for three or four years after coming into their possession, due to the speed with which competitors could propagate their own stock.[30]

What scale of enterprise was the largest nursery business? The chief means of assessing the size of businesses in the absence of annual accounts or probate inventories is to look at the insured value of fixed capital using fire insurance records.[31] In the period between 1780 and 1860 fire insurance of business premises was dominated by Sun Fire Assurance and Phoenix.[32] This discussion concentrates on London nurseries insured by Sun Fire between 1780 and 1848.[33] Loddiges' Nursery, the most prominent nursery business of its day, was insured in 1803 and 1808, and by that time, even before the construction of its largest glass houses, it ranked as one of the largest risks insured by Sun Fire. Of the remaining 200 policies also issued in 1803 only three were for larger sums – a wine merchant at Wapping, a malt distiller at Pimlico and a chemist and druggist at Cheapside.[34] Contemporaries judged

Loddiges to be the one of largest nursery businesses of its day, especially with respect to its fixed capital of glasshouses. In 1803 the business insured its glasshouses, hot houses and stove for £1,000 [£1.06 million], and the stock and utensils contained therein for the same sum.

The other larger nurseries, Archibald Thomson of Mile End and Thomas Barr of Balls Pond Road, Islington, also had substantial sums assured for rebuilding of glasshouses – £500 [£533,500] in the case of the camellia specialist Thomson and £200 [£213,400] in the case of Barr. Some insurance policies contain a breakdown of the differing premiums paid for each item insured within the policy, and it is evident from a comparison of the premiums paid on dwellings, buildings and glasshouses that nursery owners were required to pay very high premiums to insure their glasshouses, due in part to the high excise duty on glass.[35] A crude comparison of the premiums paid for buildings cover and for glasshouse cover suggests that the cost of the latter was approximately twenty times higher per pound of coverage compared to buildings cover.

Most nursery businesses in and around London were modest enterprises, with fixed capital values akin to those of small to medium farms. Agricultural buildings provide the closest comparison to nursery buildings for which capital values have been studied intensively. A small farmer's dwelling house might have an insured value of £250 [£266,700], or £1,000 [£1.06 million] for a large farm house in 1800, while the mean insured value of agricultural stock and utensils was £538 [£638,300].[36] The mean value of commercial property insured in London was £298 [£353,000], and the mean value of insured personal possessions in London was £245 [£290,700] in the period 1800–50.[37] In comparison, nursery owners in London insured their dwellings and premises for sums between £200 and £620 during the period 1780–1848, except for the Loddiges family.[38] The house of Conrad Loddiges was insured for £1,400 [£1.28 million] in 1808, on a par with many substantial London residences of the period. By 1836, George Loddiges was insuring another house at Paradise Row, just off Mare Street for £700 [£592,900], but also insuring household goods, china and glass, prints and pictures, musical instruments, and curiosities including his collection of stuffed birds, for £1,900 [£1.6 million]. This accumulation of goods reflects a prosperous middle-class lifestyle as well as the disposable income to pursue a variety of cultural and scientific interests and to amass valuable collections. Joseph Knight, George Loddiges' main competitor during this period, was sufficiently wealthy to buy a two-and-a-half-acre plot in Cadogan Street, Chelsea, in 1840, and donate it to a Catholic parish, and to build Bitham Hall, at Avon Dassett in Warwickshire, as his retirement home in 1853.[39]

A LARGE AND DIFFERENTIATED TRADE

Carving out a niche

It would be a mistake to infer from the preceding account that the nursery trade was structured in a hierarchical fashion, with a few large nurseries at the top of the chain and many smaller ones serving only their own neighbourhoods. An examination of the accounts of the fashionable Mayfair gardener and florist James Cochran for the period between 1813 and 1817 suggests that the market was instead differentiated, with a high degree of trade between businesses, which permitted a multiplicity of traders to cater to specific markets differentiated by locality and class. Cochran's business at 7 Duke Street, for example, catered to a geographically distinct clientele, the wealthy aristocratic and middle-class residents of the Mayfair streets around Grosvenor Square,[40] selling cut flowers, flower displays, contract gardening services and seeds.[41] His customers could rent flowers by the night or the week for displays during parties, usually massed in tiers to obscure the walls of the room or displayed in a conservatory built at upper ground floor level onto the back of a townhouse. Customers could also engage Cochran's men to come and plant up and maintain a flower border at their town house during the London season.[42] Cochran also supplied their needs when residing in the country, supplying large orders of vegetable seeds for their country estates.[43] Cochran himself made purchases from seedsmen such as Samuel Harrison, with whom he did substantial business.[44] He also sold seeds to a number of nurserymen who were regular customers, suggesting that the division between seedsmen, nurserymen and gardeners was far from clear cut in this period.[45] Cochran's accounts reveal an enormous breadth of suppliers – 267 in the period 1813 to 1815 – including modest trade with the most prominent exotic nurseries of the day, a substantial trade in bulbs with Dutch nurseries and regular supply of small trees and shrubs by Waterer & Co of Knap Hill, Surrey, a specialist in American plants.[46] Cochran's stock was not restricted to plants and seeds. He also sold several types of flower vase supplied by Josiah Wedgwood and held copies of William Aiton's *Hortus Kewensis* on a sale or return basis.[47] Cochran bought in large quantities of stock from nurserymen throughout the summer that were sold on to customers at a premium of up to 100 per cent.

Nursery businesses also acquired stock from nursery owners abroad. Loudon observed in 1835 that 'A number of new azaleas, and other American shrubs and trees, and new varieties of fruit trees, have been imported from Belgium; many new roses and orange trees from France; and many flowers, such as Dutch anemones, &c., from Holland'.[48] Samuel Harrison was a regular purchaser of bulbs from nurseries in Holland, while Joseph Knight purchased stock from 1814 on annual continental tours, a practice recommended to other nurserymen by the ever-improving Loudon.[49]

Commercial links

The high degree of interconnection observed in Cochran's accounts is also evident in the accounts of Samuel Harrison's nursery and in those of Colvill's Exotic Nursery. Samuel Harrison, who took over a nursery business from his uncle Henry Hewitt upon his death in 1790, concluded a partnership agreement with William Bristow in 1819, by which time the business stock was valued at £10,000 [£8.4 million]. (Harrison's Nursery was located on the site subsequently occupied by Kensington Olympia, on the north side of the road to Hammersmith.) Samuel Harrison's accounts show regular and sizeable trade with at least ten large London nurseries in the period 1809–11, including Lee and Kennedy, Colvill's Exotic Nursery, Daniel Fitch, William Malcolm, William Rollisson and Gibbs & Co, as well as substantial transactions with James Cochran,[50] and as noted previously, there was also a high degree of financial interdependence, notably between the seed merchants and nursery businesses.

In 1819 Harrison's own debts had already led one of his largest creditors, the partnership of John George and Jacob Wrench, seedsmen of Thames Street in the City of London, to require the assignment to the partners of a life assurance policy on Samuel Harrison's life for the sum of £1,000 [£844,000], as a security against his debts with the business.[51] Eventually Samuel Harrison and William Bristow were declared bankrupt in November 1832, and the assignees appointed by the creditors to oversee the winding up of the business were William Nash of The Strand, a seedsman, and John Willmott of Lewisham, a nurseryman.[52] The nature of their businesses suggest that Nash and Willmott would have been leading creditors; by this time, William Nash was one of the principal dealers in seeds in London.

Harrison's accounts reveal a range of business practices that may have contributed to his bankruptcy, especially the large amount of debt carried by the business on a seasonal basis. Harrison's nursery dealt predominantly in seeds, grown either on the nursery's own land or by farmers outside London who would ship seed to the nursery after harvesting. It also dealt in fruit trees. A substantial proportion of the firm's business was conducted with customers outside London, requiring the senior partner Samuel Harrison to spend three to four months each summer touring the country to collect debts and to solicit new orders from existing customers. These journeys were substantial financial undertakings in their own right, illustrating the scale of Harrison's enterprise at the time. His northern journey in 1807 lasted from 2 July until 27 October, with a budget of twenty-seven shillings [£1,276] per day for board, lodging and entertainment of customers, hire of a gig for eighteen weeks at one guinea a week [£992] and £54 5*s* 8*d* [£51,320] in gratuities, for receipts of £6,195 11*s* 3*d* [£5.85 million]. Gratuities, in the form of a 10 per cent commission paid to the head gardener, were a necessary business expense to achieve orders and must have provided a substantial supplement to the wages of a head gardener. The receipt of such gratuities may explain why head gardeners such as George Sinclair at Woburn Abbey were later able to buy into established nursery businesses.

Harrison also paid large bills to seed suppliers on these journeys.[53] The viability of business networks – and the consequent dissemination of goods – depended on an ability to collect debts in person if all else failed. Loudon's observation that nursery businesses were burdened by 'the very long credit generally taken by country gentlemen' is certainly borne out in examination of Harrison's accounts.[54] Harrison's most difficult and disfavoured client, Mr. Tomlin of Banbury in Oxfordshire, persistently queried his bills and paid none for four years. Eventually Harrison wrote in exasperation, 'we are at length satisfied that quibble, discontent, murmuring and procrastination are the basis on which all your commercial transactions are supported'.[55] But credit might also be extended in order to maintain the loyalty of socially prestigious customers. At the pinnacle of London society George Child Villiers, fifth Earl of Jersey, was another persistent debtor of Harrison's Nursery; by 1819 Villiers had paid no bill of Harrison's for four years.[56] Villiers was also a customer of Colvill's Exotic Nursery during the same period, but perhaps James Colvill was a more canny businessman, for the Earl of Jersey does not feature among the list of clients who had been granted prolonged credit between 1810 and 1820.[57]

GOOD AND BAD DEBT IN THE NURSERY TRADE

The management of debt and the credit that was its corollary were critical features of nineteenth-century commerce. Whereas modern businesses can finance their inventory from bank lending but impose strict credit terms on their customers, nineteenth-century businesses operated on long credit cycles with minimal bank lending to underwrite trading. Although debt might be converted into bills of exchange to generate cashflow for a business, there is no evidence that either Colvill's Nursery or Samuel Harrison were able to avail themselves of that facility.[58] The ability to manage one's debtors and creditors successfully assured the longevity of one's business, and in the nursery business management of debts appears to have been critical in determining which businesses became more prominent. In the luxury trades that catered to the aristocracy and the newly enriched, credit and debt acquired a geographical and calendrical character that mirrored the seasonal rhythm of the nursery business. One example is the need to carry out regional tours to collect debts and orders during the summer months.[59] E. J. Willson suggested that Samuel Harrison's practice of touring customers to collect debts and solicit orders was becoming dated by the 1820s due to the emergence of the printed catalogue, and risked extending unmanageable credit to existing customers, leading to Harrison's bankruptcy in 1833. Although the scale of debt carried by the business clearly grew in the 1820s, and likewise crippled many other nursery businesses, it is also the case, as previously observed, that the expansion of the provincial nursery trade challenged London businesses to specialize.[60] Competition from the provinces winnowed out those nurseries which did a bit of everything and tried to do so on a national scale. Furthermore, economic conditions were challenging for all businesses after the 1825 banking crisis, and by 1827 credit ceased to be extended to existing customers of Harrison's Nursery if bills were left unpaid.[61] Specialization in some aspect of the exotic trade was a prudent path towards maintaining a viable business, if the skills and connections required to obtain, cultivate and market exotic plants could be maintained. This imperative perhaps explains why nursery businesses tended to persist in families and die with family members too.

Prudent management – the case of Colvill's Exotic Nursery

Colvill's Exotic Nursery provides an example of a business that was prudent in the management of credit but curtailed by death. James Colvill (*c.*1746–1822) founded the business in 1783 and by 1795 it was already well known for its selection of exotic plants. The nursery was located on the north side of the King's Road on the site of what is now Anderson Street, opposite Duke of York Square. By 1811 the nursery was estimated to have between 30,000 and 40,000 square feet under glass. The nursery leased a second site at Roehampton from 1827 to 1834 but fell into decline and bankruptcy after the death of James Colvill the Younger in 1832.[62] The nursery specialized in chrysanthemums, roses and pelargoniums, along with other hothouse and greenhouse plants. It was famed for its winter displays of bulbs, many of them hybrids raised by botanist Robert Sweet, who was foreman in charge of exotic plants between 1819 and 1826.[63] While working at Colvill's nursery Sweet began to publish his series of illustrated works on exotic plants.[64]

Figure 2. Caroline Maria Applebee, *Geraniums 'Venusta', 'Formosa' and 'Barclayana' (Pelargonium), 1833. Pelargonium venustum*, featured in Robert Sweet's *Geraniaceae*, was raised from seed at Colvill's nursery in 1823. RHS Lindley Collections

Loudon praised Colvill's Nursery for the brilliance of its displays of forced flowers and bulbs and its artful planting of *Wisteria consequana* in both a heated conservatory and an unheated greenhouse to maximize the season during which visitors could enjoy the blooms and pungent scent of this recent introduction.[65] Colvill displayed orchid specimens on a tree constructed from cocoa shells and moss so that 'there is one species or another in flower every day of the year' to reward visitors, indicating the extent to which this nursery must have sought to entice visitors to visit, return regularly and develop an interest in exotics, especially the more expensive exotics such as orchids.[66]

Colvill's Nursery is the only specialist in exotic plants with surviving records.[67] These cover the periods 1809–28 and 1832–4. Descriptions of what was purchased are not included for the earlier period, though the accounts provide details of customers and major creditors, and of business expenditure. They also show sums received from named customers in cash or on account, and sums disbursed to named traders, with a note of the goods or services purchased. The earlier set of accounts also includes a running total of credit extended, with details of the terms of credit and payments on account.

The nursery's accounts show that aristocratic collectors were regular customers and were extended substantial credit to satisfy their horticultural tastes. George Spencer-Churchill, Marquess of Blandford, the heir of the Duke of Marlborough and the owner of Whiteknights, one of the most celebrated gardens of the period, appears to have been Colvill's most valuable customer after 1809 when the available details of sums on account begin. Colvill's records show that select customers with large debts to the business had structured payment terms and that these were honoured almost without exception.[68] Credit of £200 [£181,000] for eight months was extended to the marquess of Blandford in September 1809, with a further £100 [£90,480] to be paid in twelve months' time. Both debts were cleared. He received further credit of £142 2*s* 9*d* [£128,600] in March 1812 for a period of twelve months. This payment term was not honoured but in March 1815 credit of £500 [£399,400] was extended to the marquess for the period of twelve months.[69] Whether this sum consolidated the previous debt or represented completely new spending is unclear, although the Marquess was, by this stage in his career of notorious extravagance, approaching the point where he had to borrow £50,000 [£42 million] to keep his creditors at bay.[70] Lacking corresponding order records, it is not possible to say what purchases the credit covered.

This section has considered debt and the management of credit in some detail to address Loudon's claim that bad debt – and certain types of debtor – undermined the nursery business in the early nineteenth century. A geographical and calendrical pattern of debt and credit rooted in the dominance of the landed aristocracy characterized early nineteenth century businesses catering to the middle class and the aristocracy. Whereas smaller shopkeepers were beginning to move to a cash-based commercial economy by this time,[71] the business cycle for many trades catering to the landed classes continued to operate to an agricultural and aristocratic calendar, imposing stresses on smaller businesses. Taken together, these factors indicate a well-established trade with a high degree of integration. Taking advantage of new opportunities to serve customers in the early nineteenth century allowed nurseries to move beyond their immediate locales and clientele to make exotic plants available to a wider range of customers and made businesses less reliant on a small number of wealthy customers. These innovations are reviewed in the next section.

RETAILERS AND CUSTOMERS

Distribution

What Jon Stobart, Andrew Hann and Victoria Morgan have described as the 'spatiality of consumption' – the ways in which businesses and customers engaged with each other across space to create new opportunities for consumption – expanded greatly in the nursery trade in the early-nineteenth century. The retailing of plants extended beyond the shop to engage customers in a range of spatial arrangements that reflected innovations in transport and communications in this period. In common with other areas of retailing, the nursery trade underwent considerable transformation in response to urbanization and the expansion of a middle class of means beyond London. The proliferation of specialized shops in the capital during the eighteenth century reflected the concentration of population and wealth necessary to support those businesses.[72] But an examination of the nursery trade allows us to see that the spatial boundaries of urban consumption extended beyond the town and its inhabitants.[73] Although by no means the only business area taking advantage of innovations in communications during the early part of the nineteenth century, the expansion of nursery businesses was aided by improvements that greatly increased their potential reach.[74] Mail coaches, the expansion of the canal system, cheaply printed catalogues, the expanding postal service and the railway transport of commercial goods were all employed in the marketing of nurserymen's products, while a new urban shopping culture of display and personal service was embraced by the larger nursery owners as they competed for wealthy customers. An expanding middle class, the building of suburbs where houses with gardens were the norm and the increasing range of horticultural publications all stimulated demand for plants, trees and shrubs. Nursery businesses in the early nineteenth century usually combined a face-to-face and a mail order clientele. Business outside London was serviced by stagecoach in the main prior to the arrival of the railways and the penny post. The improvement of the road system and the expansion of stagecoach services made it practical for businesses to ship goods further and faster by 1800.[75] Goods would be dispatched to customers and seeds and other items would be sent by suppliers in the same way. To fulfil an order for pineapple plants, for example, Samuel Harrison requested the gardener at Mrs. Tudway's house in Wells, Somerset, to send ten pine plants by stagecoach, indicating not only the use of specialist suppliers but also the way in which private gardens with specialist collections far from London might service the nursery trade.[76] Larger items would be sent by horse and cart to a location – often a coaching inn – that could be reached in half a day from London, at which the customer would be expected to attend with their own transport to complete the delivery. To deliver twenty fruiting pineapple plants to Lady and Viscount Hampden at Glynde Place in Sussex, for example, Harrison asked for a covered wagon to meet his team at East Grinstead.[77] Goods might also be sent by water; John Harvey suggested that large quantities of young trees could be shipped by canal from London to the Midlands and Manchester, and although Harrison used canal shipping from London for some goods, there is also evidence that he used carriers who conveyed goods by ship to Gainsborough, the furthest navigable point on the River Trent, before sending them on by canal to Loughborough. Vessels travelling to Gainsborough advertised onward shipment by canal to destinations throughout the Midlands as far as Wolverhampton, Liverpool and Manchester, and to Yorkshire too.[78] At least one nursery adapted its techniques of culture specifically to cater to the mail order trade in this period; Dennis & Co, a specialist in pelargoniums, propagated its cuttings in very small clay pots called 'thumbs', 'for the convenience of sending to a distance in little bulk', and maintained stock of 15,000–20,000 plants in the summer months.[79]

Catalogues

Harrison's business correspondence does not discuss postal charges or the use of postal services to distribute seeds, but within months of the inauguration of the Uniform Penny Post in 1840, Loudon was enthusiastically promoting it as a boon to horticulture. Prior to its introduction, merchants such as Harrison might send notices of new stock with bills to existing customers, but tradesmen's circulars were a source of nuisance to many because the recipient was required to pay for the item according to the distance it had travelled. Praising the possibilities of the new postal system, Loudon observed:

> Collectors of plants receiving such catalogues, when they see a kind mentioned in them of which they are doubtful, may write for a specimen, or for a scion, or for seeds. Another great advantage of the system is, that by means of the adhesive stamp the sender of a letter may not only pay it, but enclose a stamp in order to pay the answer, and thus make sure of it.[80]

The new postal system aided circulation of information and goods, and nurserymen quickly seized the opportunities presented for promotion and supply of their goods by post, contriving entirely new marketing methods and products. Within months of praising the new postal system, Loudon reported that from 'Messrs. Sang of Kirkcaldy we received a prepaid packet very neatly done up, containing the seeds of 12 kinds of annuals, each with the name printed, and the price of the whole 12 only 1*s* [£43]'. He concluded: 'If this does not lead to the general distribution of every useful and ornamental plant of which seeds are procurable, the fault will be in the public, not in government'.[81]

Printed catalogues began to be issued more often by nursery businesses in the 1820s and 1830s as printing costs declined. Catalogues of businesses dealing in exotic plants used Latin plant names to indicate botanical accuracy, but this did not always resolve two frequent criticisms levelled at the trade, the misclassification of plants grown from seed and the mistaken attribution of plants based on a lack of knowledge of botanical reference specimens and authorities. Loudon complained of catalogues in 1840:

> We wish every nurseryman would get into the habit of putting authorities after his scientific names; and also of making certain that his names are correct, by comparing his plants (by specimens or otherwise) with those of some nursery or botanic garden where the names are acknowledged to be so.[82]

Whereas catalogues of the early-eighteenth century might contain illustrations,[83] those of the early nineteenth century increasingly relied upon Latin terminology and the supportive illustrated botanical literature of the period such as *Curtis's Botanical Magazine* to assist prospective purchasers in making their choices. Potential buyers were assumed to be sufficiently educated in taxonomy to be able to locate the types of plants they wanted. Loddiges' catalogues, for example, became progressively more organized by taxonomy. Whereas an 1804 catalogue was organized into lists of hardy perennials, greenhouse plants and stove plants, by the 1840s the firm was issuing separate catalogues covering stove and greenhouse plants, orchids and palms, reflecting not only the growth in its stock but also the increasing specialism of some gardeners and collectors. Within these catalogues, lists were organized by genus, indicating the degree of specialist knowledge customers were expected to possess.[84] On the other hand, nurseries selling native trees and plants, especially annuals, continued to use English names in their catalogues, suggesting the distinction in education and knowledge drawn between patrons of the two types of business.[85]

Unlike late-nineteenth-century catalogues, which included price lists, nursery catalogues of the early-nineteenth century almost always omitted prices.[86] John Harvey has argued that at the top end of the market, at least, to mention prices would have appeared ungentlemanly.[87] Prior to the introduction of the penny post, catalogues would have been mailed to existing customers or requested by prospective customers, and as Samuel Harrison's letter book shows, these lists, whether handwritten or printed, often formed the basis for a correspondence through which the nursery owner established the customer's needs and their capacity to pay. The availability of new catalogues was also advertised in the horticultural press. Loddiges' Nursery issued regular catalogues from 1777 and began to issue catalogues for specialities such as palms and orchids from the 1830s.

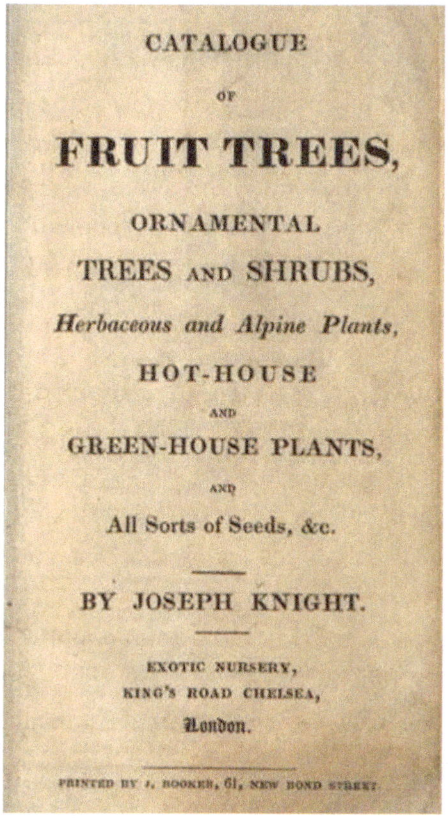
CATALOGUE

OF

FRUIT TREES,

ORNAMENTAL

TREES AND SHRUBS,

Herbaceous and Alpine Plants,

HOT-HOUSE

AND

GREEN-HOUSE PLANTS,

AND

All Sorts of Seeds, &c.

BY JOSEPH KNIGHT.

EXOTIC NURSERY,
KING'S ROAD CHELSEA,
London.

PRINTED BY J. HOOKER, 61, NEW BOND STREET.

Figure 3. Joseph Knight's catalogue, c. 1808. RHS Lindley Collections

Shopping in person

Shopping in person remained the most important means by which customers viewed and acquired exotic plants (Figure 4). Nursery visits had become an accepted form of polite and improving recreation by the 1790s when William Curtis established his Botanic Garden in Sloane Street. By the 1820s, Loudon's regular columns in *The Gardener's Magazine* on nursery visits in London and beyond drew attention to seasonal and novel attractions. Nurseries offered a spectacular experience of flowering plants, exotics and controlled climates. They also attracted the passing visitor through external displays; on the King's Road, Dennis & Co cultivated dahlias on an acre adjoining the road and a further piece of ground 'fortunately adjoining the Fulham Road'.[88] Contemporary visitors have left no accounts of the practical aspects of their visits, as opposed to what they saw during their visit, but nurserymen were accustomed to receiving visitors and answering detailed botanical and horticultural questions.[89] Although gardeners might make selections on behalf of their employers, their employers appear to have visited the nursery and different family members were equally responsible for making purchases.[90] The accounts of James Colvill's Exotic Nursery show that many purchases were made in person, by the gentry, by aristocrats, and almost as frequently by women as by men. At Colvill's nursery women bought cut flowers and nosegays but were less likely to buy shrubs. Substantial orders that imply a new garden, or remodelling of an existing garden, were invariably ascribed to male customers. Trade followed the social as well as the gardening calendar: in 1812, for example, orders at Colvill's Exotic Nursery were highest in May (£543 18*s* 6*d*) [£440,000] and lowest in September (£75) [£61,230] and December (£94) [£76,740], with flowers the biggest source of income during the winter months. Both Colvill's and James Cochran's accounts show a marked reduction in business activity from the end of the London season in late July until mid-February and a lower frequency of purchases by titled customers during this period.[91] During the London season from February to July around one-third of Colvill's customers were titled and included some of the most illustrious names in London's social and political life.[92] These included Sir David Dundas, commander-in-chief of the army at this time; Lord Liverpool (secretary of war and the colonies) and the Dowager Lady Liverpool; Lord Grosvenor, the developer of the Grosvenor estate; the Duchess of Devonshire and numerous other aristocrats.

Figure 4. A customer and nurseryman at 'Loddige's Palmarum', *Pictorial Times*, 10 October 1846

Colvill's accounts show that the lifeblood of his business was cut flowers – his business was celebrated for forcing flowers and bulbs under glass, as previously mentioned – and the sale of nosegays, small sweet-scented bouquets. Despite proclaiming his business an 'Exotic' nursery, most of the named plants that Colvill sold were common European plants such as laurels and lavender. The most frequently sold exotic plants were American plants such as *Yucca filamentosa, Yucca gloriosa, Eschscholzia californica* (the California poppy), *Kalmia latifolia* (mountain laurel) and *Kalmia angustifolia*, and the recent Chinese introductions *Magnolia conspicua*, *Magnolia purpurea*, China roses and, most popular of all, *Aucuba japonica* (Japanese or spotted laurel).[93] The only hybrid varieties detectable from Colvill's order books were Archibald Thomson's *Magnolia* x. *Thomsoniae* and *Magnolia* x. *Soulangeana*.[94] Sales followed a seasonal rhythm that would be recognizable to any nursery or garden centre today: peonies, rhododendons and magnolia sold well in their spring flowering season, delphiniums in June, yuccas, roses and dahlias and geraniums in July and August, and shrubs for autumn planting in November.

PRICES PAID FOR PLANTS

The accounts of Samuel Harrison and Colvill's Exotic Nursery provide some evidence regarding the value placed on specific plants and give some indication of how much exotic plants cost and whether they could be considered luxury goods. Colvill's accounts show that items of the same size had a standard price which was the same for all customers. Where a lower price was charged for an item the cash book distinguishes that this was a smaller item. This implies that where nurseries did not publish their prices, they did so not because they expected to bargain with customers, but because they did not wish to run to the expense of reprinting catalogues if prices changed. Table 1 shows the comparative prices charged by four businesses – Colvill's Exotic Nursery, Harrison's Nursery, Messrs. Loddiges and Caldwell's Nursery of Knutsford, Cheshire, as a regional comparator.

Table 1.
Comparative prices of common exotics.

	Colvill	Harrison	Caldwell	Loddiges
Yucca filamentosa	1*s* 6*d* [£66] (1834a)[95]	n/a	1*s* 6*d* [£65] (1832)[96]	n/a
Yucca gloriosa	5*s* [£221] (1834b)[97]	n/a	3*s* 6*d* [£151] (1832)	n/a
Magnolia conspicua	3*s* 6*d* [£155] (1834a&b)	n/a	7*s* 6*d* [£321] (1830)[98]	n/a
Magnolia purpurea	5*s* [£221] (1834a)	n/a	1*s* 6*d*–2*s* 6*d* [£65–£108] (1832)	n/a
Magnolia 3ft	n/a	7*s* 6*d* [£316] (1819)[99]	n/a	n/a
Camellia japonica	n/a	£1 1*s* [£857] (1812)[100]	n/a	n/a
Strelitzia regina	n/a	£4 4*s* [£3,429] (1812)	n/a	£5 10*s* 9*d* [£4,679] (1820)[101]
Escholzia [sic] *californica*	9*d* [£33] (1834a)	n/a	6*d*–1*s* [£21–£43] (1832)	n/a

	Colvill	Harrison	Caldwell	Loddiges
Kalmia latifolia	3*s* 6*d* [£155] (1834b)	2*s* 6*d* [£102] (1812)	2*s*–7*s* 6*d* [£86–£325] (1832)	7*s* 6*d* [£316] (1820)
Kalmia angustifolia	3*s* 6*d* [£155] (1834b)	n/a	4*s* 6*d* [£328] (1791)[102] 1*s*–2*s* 6*d* [£43–£108] (1832)	2*s* 6*d* [£105] (1820)
Chrysanthemum (plants or stools)	9*d* [£33] (1834b)	6*d* [£20] (1812)	1*s* [£43] (1832)	n/a
Dahlia (plants or tubers)	6*d* [£22] (1834a)	7s 6d [£316] (1819)	2*s*–8*s* [£86–£347] (1832)	no price (1820)

Attempts to compare prices of another era with today's costs using the Consumer Price Index fall foul of changes in the supply of underlying commodities and technologies that give rise to the price of goods and give little sense of the historical context of prices.[103] In particular, the period between 1815 and 1835 saw a gradual deflation in all living costs apart from rent but little growth in real wages for manual work.[104] It is sounder to compare contemporary prices in the context of income and earnings. Considering wages, most of the people paid to raise these plants at Colvill's Nursery were paid between 12*s* 6*d* and 14*s* a week in 1831 [£538–£603].[105] Industrial wages in Lancashire were higher; perhaps as high as 33*s* a week [£1,422] for men working in cotton mills.[106] A comfortable middle-class living required at least £250 [£215,000] a year in the 1830s to meet the costs of servants, clothing and higher-quality household goods befitting the social status of the gentry or professional people.[107] Wax candles, for example, cost around 3*s* 3*d* a dozen [£140] and coffee 3*s* 6*d* a pound in 1830 [£150],[108] while a copy of *The Gardener's Magazine* cost 5*s* at its launch in 1826 [£216], and books such as Loudon's *Encyclopaedia of Gardening* cost £2 10*s* [£2,289]. In comparison, Colvill's Nursery charged 1*s* 6*d* for a *Yucca filamentosa*, 5*s* for a *Yucca gloriosa*, 5*s* for a *Magnolia purpurea* and 9*d* for chrysanthemum plants in 1834; and where other nursery businesses have prices available for these items, they were broadly similar in the 1830s (see Table 1 for price conversions).[109] A large nursery in Cheshire, Caldwell's of Knutsford, charged similar prices to those of Colvill's Nursery and Harrison's Nursery for the same plants, suggesting that there was no London premium and nor were provincial nurseries charging higher prices due to lack of local competition.[110]

The high prices of some items identified from nursery records, such as *Strelitzia regina,* the bird of paradise plant (£4 4*s* at Harrison's Nursery in 1812 and £5 10*s* 9*d* at Loddiges in 1820),[111] indicate the rarity and the cost of cultivation, whereas the comparative cheapness of dahlia tubers or plants indicates the relative ease of propagation and the greater supply of these items over time. Harrison's Nursery charged 7*s* 6*d* for dahlia plants in 1819, by 1832 the cheapest plants offered by Caldwell's Nursery had fallen in price to 2*s*, and there is some evidence that the prices of all items fell over time.[112] The lack of extensive price series for multiple nurseries in the early nineteenth century makes it difficult to draw firm conclusions about the relationship between dates of introductions and the trajectory of prices, or to discern whether the prices of plants followed changes in prices and incomes in the wider economy. Nevertheless, the prices charged for most of the plants sold by the nurseries discussed in this paper would not have been out of the reach of middle-class customers, particularly considering that most of the plants identified were perennial or greenhouse plants intended to form a major feature of a collection. However, as with cultural products such as books and plays, analysed by Robert D. Hume, the small size of the middle-class able to pay these sums and the frequency with which these expenditures could be borne needs to be taken into consideration.[113] Using the average earnings index to calculate present-day equivalent prices, it is clear that even the cheapest of these plants represented a more substantial investment for nineteenth-century consumers than they would for today's gardener. The expansion of the market, demonstrated by the growth in nursery businesses, was a consequence of the growth of the middle class and increases in disposable income, as well as a greater interest in the creation of gardens in new suburbs. If plants became cheaper during the first half of the nineteenth century, the prices of most plants identified in this account nevertheless placed them firmly in the category of elite goods.

CONCLUSION

An extensive nursery trade differentiated by speciality, services, neighbourhood and clientele was well established in London by the early nineteenth century. Provincial nurseries were becoming more numerous and able to supply a wider range of needs, offering greater competition to the London nurseries and perhaps stimulating a drive towards specialization that coincided with the greater availability of exotics. For a few businesses with links to scientific circles, which had the wherewithal to engage collectors and with enough surplus to invest in greenhouses and heating, specialization provided the opportunity to build substantial and profitable businesses. The place of the nursery trade and commercial collectors in the history of botany remains underappreciated. This paper provides a context for further investigations of the interactions between commerce and science in the first half of the nineteenth century, by examining the structure of the trade and its economy.

The fact that almost none of the businesses described in this paper persisted more than one or two generations beyond the original founders suggests the extent to which they depended on the skills, drive and personality of the owner. Nevertheless, this paper has shown that the trade was sufficiently diverse, interconnected and widely distributed to permit widespread commercial dissemination of the techniques necessary to raise exotic introductions. Nursery business records, despite their limited survival, demonstrate that nursery owners dealt directly with a broad array of the British aristocracy, albeit as tradesmen. Nursery businesses were among the trades which prospered in the period between 1780 and 1860 due to the demand for novelties, for luxury goods, and for consumption which demonstrated participation in polite society. The intermediary status of nursery owners made them peculiarly sensitive to the aspirations of the emerging middle class on the one hand, and the social expectations of the aristocracy and gentry on the other.

REFERENCES

[1] London, British Library, Additional MS. 31127, 'William Cobbett, Letters to America 1825–1827', fo. 19r, William Cobbett to James Cobbett, 7 Feb. 1821 (this series contains letters commencing in 1820).
[2] Brit. Library, Add. MS. 31127, 'Cobbett', fos. 25r, 37r, 50r, 57r. See also James Grande, 'William Cobbett's correspondence, 1800–1835' (unpublished doctoral thesis, University of Oxford, 2011), pp. 100–4.
[3] For *Magnolia glauca*, see Brit. Library., Add. MS. 31127, 'Cobbett', fo. 59r, 11 July 1825. Cobbett was not the first to introduce these trees but was probably among the first to attempt to cultivate the trees from seed at scale.
[4]G. D. H. Cole, *The Life of William Cobbett* (Abingdon: Routledge, 2010), p. 19. Amidst his political activities and publishing of the *Political Register*, Cobbett found time to write an extremely practical and detailed guide, *The*

English Gardener (London, 1829), to provide instructions on how to cultivate kitchen and ornamental gardens, as well as a guide to managing a smallholding, *Cottage Economy* (London, 1822), and *Woodlands* (London, 1825), a guide to trees and their management.

[5] Cobbett's nursery remained in business until 1831 when he decided to consolidate his farming and horticultural activities on a farm at Ash in Surrey, not for financial reasons but due to the pressures of his political career.

[6] *Gardener's Magazine* (*G.M.*), 11 (1835), pp. 621–2. The fall in the price of trees occurred from the 1780s onwards due to large-scale propagation by nurseries outside London to satisfy the national demand for tree planting and improvement of estates (see J. H. Harvey, 'The supply of plants in the north-west', *Garden History*, 6 (1978), pp. 33–7, at p. 36; Stephen Daniels, 'The political iconography of woodland in later Georgian England', in Denis. Cosgrove and Stephen Daniels (eds), *The Iconography of Landscape: Essays on the Symbolic Representation, Design and Use of Past Environments* (Cambridge: Cambridge University Press, 1988); Paul Elliott, Stephen Daniels and Charles Watkins, *The British Arboretum: Trees, Science and Culture in the Nineteenth Century* (London: Routledge, 2012), pp. 17, 158–62).

[7] *G.M.*, 11 (1835), pp. 621–2.

[8] For further discussion of British engagement with non-native flora through colonizing, trade and exploration, see Alan Bewell, 'Erasmus Darwin's cosmopolitan nature', *ELH (English Literary History)*, 76 (2009), pp. 19–48; Beth Fowkes Tobin, *Colonizing Nature: the Tropics in British Arts and Letters, 1760–1820* (Philadelphia, PA.: University of Pennsylvania Press 2005), esp. ch. 6; Miles Ogborn, 'Vegetable empire', in H. Curry and others (eds), *Worlds of Natural History*, (Cambridge: Cambridge University Press, 2018), pp. 271-286; Kathleen S. Murphy, 'A slaving surgeon's collection: the pursuit of natural history through the British slave trade to Spanish America', in Adriana Craciun and Mary Terrall (eds.), *Curious Encounters: Voyaging, Collecting and Making Knowledge in the Long Eighteenth Century*, ed. (Toronto: University of Toronto Press, 2019), pp. 138–58; Richard Drayton, *Nature's Government: Science, Imperial Britain and the 'Improvement of the World'* (New Haven and London: Yale University Press, 2000).

[9] For recent examinations of the relationship between botanical science and commerce in the 18th century, see Richard Coulton, 'Curiosity, commerce and conversation: nursery-gardens and nurserymen in eighteenth-century London', *London Journal*, 43 (2018), pp. 17–35; Richard Coulton, 'Curiosity, commerce, and conversation in the writing of London horticulturists during the early-eighteenth century' (unpublished doctoral thesis, Queen Mary, University of London, 2015); Sarah Easterby-Smith, *Cultivating Commerce: Cultures of Botany in Britain and France, 1760–1815* (Cambridge: Cambridge University Press, 2017).

[10] Margot Finn has previously analysed the ways in which practices of credit informed judgements and construction of character in the 19th century, see Margot Finn, *The Character of Credit: Personal Debt in English Culture, 1740–1914* (Cambridge: Cambridge University Press, 2003). Nancy Cox has examined the ways in which shop debt was managed in 17th- and 18th-century retailing, see Nancy Cox, *The Complete Tradesman: a Study of Retailing, 1550–1820* (Aldershot: Ashgate, 2000), pp. 146–62.

[11] For exceptions, see Douglas Chambers, *The Planters of the English Landscape Garden* (New Haven and London: Yale University Press, 1993); John Harvey, *Early Nurserymen* (London: Phillimore, 1974); E. J. Willson, *James Lee and the Vineyard Nursery Hammersmith* (London: Hammersmith Local History Group, 1961); E. J. Willson, *West London Nursery Gardens* (London: Fulham and Hammersmith Historical Society, 1982); David Marsh, 'The gardens and gardeners of later Stuart London' (unpublished doctoral thesis, Birkbeck University of London, 2005); Margaret Maddison, 'The Callenders, eighteenth-century northern nurserymen and seedsmen', *Garden History*, 33:2 (2005), pp. 210–224; Joy Uings, Barbara. Moth and Moira Stevenson, *Caldwell's, Nurserymen of Knutsford for Two Centuries* (Sale, 2016); Joy Uings, 'Gardens and gardening in a fast-changing urban environment: Manchester 1750–1850' (unpublished doctoral thesis, Manchester Metropolitan University, 2013); Fiona Davison, *The Hidden Horticulturists: the Untold Story of the Men Who Shaped Britain's Gardens* (London: Atlantic, 2019), pp. 206–40; Roderick Floud, *An Economic History of the English Garden* (London: Allen Lane, 2019), pp. 126–58.

[12] Kathleen Clark, 'What the nurserymen did for us: the roles and influence of the nursery trade on the landscapes and gardens of the eighteenth century', *Garden History*, 40:1 (2012), pp. 17–33.

[13] Malcolm Thick, 'Market gardening in England and Wales', in Joan Thirsk (ed.) *The Agrarian History of England and Wales*: volume V (Cambridge: Cambridge University Press, 1985), pp. 503–32 (p. 526); John Harvey, *Early Gardening Catalogues* (London: Phillimore, 1972), p. 14; Harvey, *Early Nurserymen*; Floud, pp. 126–57.

[14] For specialization in the 18th-century nursery trade, see Coulton, 'Curiosity', pp. 24–31; Easterby-Smith, pp. 21–45.

[15] John Harvey, 'The nurseries on Milne's land-use map', *Transactions of the London and Middlesex Archaeological Society*, 24 (1973), pp. 177–98.

[16] *Post Office London Directory, 1841 (Part 1: Street, Commercial, & Trades Directories)* (London, 1841), pp. 768–9.

[17] For further discussion of the role of women in the nursery trade in this period, see Dianne Barre, 'Enterprising women: shaping the business of gardening in the Midlands 1780–1830', in Malcolm Dick and Elaine Mitchell (eds), *Gardens and Green Spaces in the West Midlands since 1700* (Hatfield: West Midlands Publications, 2018), pp. 102–19; Easterby-Smith, pp. 45–9.

[18] 'Economic history: farm-gardening and market gardening', in Patricia Croot (ed), *Victoria County History of Middlesex*: *Volume 12*: *Chelsea*, (London: Victoria County History, 2004), pp. 150–5 (*British History Online* <http://www.british-history.ac.uk/vch/middx/vol12/pp150-155> [accessed 14 Nov. 2017]).

[19] Ronald Webber, *The Early Horticulturists* (Newton Abbott: David & Charles, 1968), p. 23.

[20] Willson, *West London Nursery Gardens*, pp. 36, 48, 94–5; *V.C.H. Middlesex*, *Vol. 12*., p.150; *Johnstone's London Commercial Directory and Street Guide* (London, 1818), p. 283.

[21] Webber, *Early Horticulturists,* p. 27.

[22] James Mangles, *The Floral Calendar, Monthly and Daily. With Miscellaneous Details Relative to Plants and Flowers, Gardens and Greenhouses, Horticulture and Botany, Aviaries, &c. &c,* (London, 1839), p. 96.

[23] J. Middleton, *View of the Agriculture of Middlesex* (London, 1798), p. 272.

[24] Prices in this paper have been converted to 2019 values using the average earnings index maintained by *Measuring Worth*, consistent with Roderick Floud's recommendation. See Floud, p. 12; 'Five ways to compute the relative value of a U.K. pound amount, 1270 to present,' *Measuring Worth*, 2020 <http://www.measuringworth.com/ukcompare/> [accessed 20 July 2020].

[25] G.B.G. Bull, 'Thomas Milne's Land Utilization Map of the London Area in 1800', *The Geographical Journal*, 22.1 (1956), pp. 25-30 (p. 25).

[26] Mangles, *Floral Calendar* p. 97.

[27] Mangles, *Floral Calendar,* pp. 98–100.

[28] Harvey, *Early Gardening Catalogues* (1972), pp. 49–51, 56–7.

[29] *G.M.*, 8 (1832), 130.

[30] *G.M.*, viii (1832), 130.

[31] David Marsh used probate inventories to characterize the Stuart-era gardening trade in London, but by the early 19th century probate inventories were rare, leaving no information regarding business sizes in the testamentary sources consulted (Marsh, *Gardens and Gardeners*, pp. 380–96).

[32] D. T. Jenkins, 'The practice of insurance against fire, 1750–1840, and historical research', in Oliver Westall, *The Historian and the Business of Insurance* (Manchester: Manchester University Press, 1984), pp. 9–38, (p. 12).

[33] Sun Fire records are indexed by the name of the policy holder to 1848, whereas Phoenix records require a policy number or an approximate renewal date to locate details of a specific business. In the absence of such information, this discussion covers Sun Fire records only.

[34] London Metropolitan Archives (L.M.A.), Sun Insurance Company Registers, CLC/B/192/F/001/MS11936/427/745555; CLC/B/192/F/001/MS11936/427/745556; CLC/B/192/F/001/MS11936/427/745563. From 1808 Sun Fire imposed a ceiling of £3,000 on extra-hazardous risks, which may have set Loddiges Nursery outside normal arrangements owing to numerous stoves and boilers on the premises. Insurance of larger enterprises was commonly split between insurers (see H. A. L. Cockerell and Edwin Green, *The British Insurance Business: a Guide to its History and Records. Second Edition* (Sheffield: Sheffield Academic Press, 1994), pp. 31–3, 48.

[35] Business premises were exempt from the window tax which remained in force until 1847, but excise duty on glass – a separate tax – was approximately twice the cost of production. The abolition of excise duty in 1845 halved the cost of glass for all uses (see Theodore Barker, *The Glassmakers. Pilkington: the Rise of an International Company 1826–1976* (London: Weidenfeld and Nicholson, 1977), pp. 29, 59, 78).

[36] Charles Feinstein and Sidney Pollard, *Studies in Capital Formation in the United Kingdom, 1750–1920* (Oxford: Oxford University Press, 1988), pp. 14–15, 254.

[37] Feinstein and Pollard, *Capital Formation*, pp. 253, 256.

[38] Many of the properties insured were on the outskirts of London in locations beginning to be encroached upon by housing development in the early 19th century, such as Hackney, Kensington and Islington, hence the comparison with agricultural rather than manufacturing property costs, where the residence was also less likely to be co-located with the business premises by this period.

[39] Warwickshire Gardens Trust, *Bitham Hall, Avon Dassett, Warwickshire: a Brief History* (Warwick: Warwickshire Gardens Trust, 2001).

[40] For discussion of the evolution of this neighbourhood and the trades that serviced it, see Hannah Greig, *The Beau Monde: Fashionable Society in Georgian London* (Oxford: Oxford University Press, 2013).

[41]The National Archives (T.N.A.), C 111/132, Day Book 1816. See also Todd Longstaffe-Gowan, *The London Town Garden, 1740–1840* (New Haven and London: Yale University Press, 2001).

[42] T.N.A., C 111/132, Day Book 1817; C 111/133, Ledger 1815–16. In June 1816, the Duke of Grafton was charged £7 16*s* for the hire of 104 plants for a week and a further 21*s* a week for five weeks of continuing hire. See also Longstaffe-Gowan, *The London Town Garden*, pp. 167, 169, 173.

[43] The business fulfilled very large orders of vegetable and flower seed between Jan. and March 1817, in preparation for sowing time, to Lord Leveson Gower (£11 7*s* 2*d*), Lord Eardley (£23 1*s* 6*d*), the Earl of Stair (£43 7*s* 5*d*) and again in the first three months of 1818 and 1819, and to other customers outside London. See T.N.A., C 111/132, Day Book 1816–17.

[44] T.N.A., C 111/133, Ledger 1813–15. Cochrane owed Harrison £272 3*s* 4*d* in Feb. 1812; Harrison was his largest supplier of seeds in this period.

[45] T.N.A., C 111/132, Day Book, 1818.

[46] T.N.A., C 111/133, Ledger 1813–15.

[47] T.N.A., C 111/133, Ledger 1813–15. See also T.N.A., C 111/133, Ledger 1821.

[48] *G.M.*, 11 (1835), p. 622.

[49] *G.M.*, 9 (1834), p.12.

[50] L.M.A., B/HRS/03, Account Book, 1809–11.

[51] L.M.A., B/HRS/387, Assignment for a Life Assurance for the Sum of £1,000 to Jacob George and John Wrench, 1 Jan. 1819.

[52] L.M.A., B/HRS/389, Assignment of a Life Interest in a Moiety of 3 Leasehold Messuages; *The London Gazette*, 19011, p. 66, 8 Jan. 1833. Although the appointment of official assignees by the Lord Chancellor to manage bankrupt's estate was introduced in 1831, to combat fraud and incompetence in the voluntary assignment of a bankrupt's estate in London creditors' assignees continued to play a part in proceedings. See V. Markham Lester, *Victorian Insolvency: Bankruptcy, Imprisonment, and Company Winding-Up in Nineteenth-Century England* (Oxford: Clarendon Press, 1995), pp. 44–7.

[53] L.M.A., B/HRS/03, Account Book.

[54] *G.M.*, 11 (1835), pp. 621–2.

[55] L.M.A. B/HRS/013, Letter Book 1818–19, fo. 196r.

[56] L.M.A. B/HRS/013, Letter Book 1818–19, Samuel Harrison to Lord Jersey, 20 June 1819, fo. 115r. The fifth Earl of Jersey followed in his father's footsteps: the fourth earl had been threatened with imprisonment in 1802 for his unpaid debts (see H. E. Maxwell, 'George Bussy Villiers, fourth Earl of Jersey (1735–1805)', *Oxford Dictionary of National Biography* (2004) <https://www.oxforddnb.com/view/10.1093/ref:odnb/9780198614128.001.0001/odnb-9780198614128-e-28295> [accessed 10 Aug. 2020]).

[57] Lambeth Archives (L.A.), Colville Family Estate, IV/39/1.

[58] Bills of exchange began to come into more general use after the financial crisis of 1825 so the lack of evidence of use probably indicates that these businesses were not among the early adopters of these instruments (see Mary Poovey, *Genres of the Credit Economy: Mediating Value in Eighteenth- and Nineteenth Century Britain* (Chicago, Ill: Chicago University Press, 2008), pp. 36–42).

[59] It is unclear from William Cobbett's *Rural Rides* if some journeys were undertaken in connection with the business of his seed farm and whether Cobbett was engaged in debt collection and order-taking. G. D. H. Cole remarked that Cobbett's rural rides mixed business with pleasure and Cobbett's accounts of his journeys are often vague regarding his actual object at a destination. For an exception suggesting that his purpose was business, see W. Cobbett, *Rural Rides* (2 vols., London: Dent, 1912), volume 2, p. 19.

[60] Willson, *West London Nursery Gardens*, p. 81; Harvey, *Early Nurserymen*, p. 10.

[61] L.M.A., B/HRS/013, fo. 297r, Samuel Harrison to John Watson. See also Boyd Hilton*, A Mad, Bad and Dangerous People? England 1783–1846* (Oxford: Oxford University Press, 2006), pp. 398–9.

[62] *V.C.H. Middlesex*, volume 12. 150–5.

[63] *G.M.*, 1 (1826), p. 31; see also *G.M.*, 5 (1829), p. 220.

[64] *G.M.*, 11 (1835), p. 159. Robert Sweet, *Geraniaceae* (London, 1820–8); *The British Flower Garden* (London, 1822); *Cistineae* (London, 1825–30); *The Botanical Cultivator* (London, 1821); *The Florist's Guide* (London, 1827–32); *Flora Australasica* (5 vols., London, 1827–8).

[65] Formerly *Glycine sinensis*, now *Wisteria sinensis*. See *G.M.*, 5 (1829), p. 339.

[66] *G.M.*, 5 (1829), p. 339.

[67] L.A., Colville Family Estate, IV/39. The nursery records appear to have survived as part of the papers of the Colville estate, from which James Colvill leased the site of his nursery. Colvill was not a member of this family. The nursery business was gradually wound up after the death of James Colvill the younger in 1832.

[68] Colvill's account book shows the repayment terms for these sums, with the note of the debt struck through in red upon repayment, a note of the date and the name of the banker who had issued the draft and confirmation that it had been honoured (see L.A., Colville Family Estate, IV/39).

[69] L.A., Colville Family Estate, IV/39.

[70] Ian Cooke, 'Whiteknights and the Marquis of Blandford', *Garden History*, 20:1 (1992), pp. 28–44 (p. 37).

[71] Helen Berry, 'Polite consumption: shopping in eighteenth- century England', *Transactions of the Royal Historical Society*, 6th ser., 12 (2002), pp. 375–94 (p. 92).

[72] Floud, pp. 133–6.

[73] John Stobart, Andrew Hann and Victoria Morgan (eds), *Spaces of Consumption: Leisure and Shopping in the English Town, c.1680–1830* (London: Routledge, 2007), pp. 18–22.

[74] N. Thrift, 'Transport and communication 1730–1914', in R. A. Dodgshon and R. A. Butlin (eds.), *An Historical Geography of England and Wales, 1730–1914* (London: Academic Press, 1990), pp. 453–86.

[75] Philip Bagwell, *The Transport Revolution from 1770* (London: Barnes & Noble, 1974).

[76] L.M.A., B/HRS/013, fos. 105r–106r, fo. 129r.

[77] L.M.A., B/HRS/013, fo. 112r.

[78] L.M.A., B/HRS/013, fo. 133r; Harrison asked for a large order of peas to be sent 'by the most ready water conveyance' from Faringdon, then in Berkshire; J. H. Harvey, 'The supply of plants in the north-west', *Garden History*, 6:3 (1978), pp. 33–7 (p. 36). Harrison also shipped trees to William Gaunt in Loughborough (see L.M.A., B/HRS/95 and 96).

[79] *G.M.*, 7 (1831), pp. 37–8. Thumb pots were the size of a thumb.

[80] *G.M.*, 6 (new ser.) (1840), pp. 96–7.

[81] *G.M.*, 6 (new ser.) (1840), pp. 268.

[82] G.M., 6 (new ser.) (1840), pp. 605.

[83] Malcolm Thick, 'Garden seeds in England in the eighteenth century – II: the trade in seeds to 1760', *Agricultural History Review*, 38 (1990), pp. 105–16.

[84] Society of Antiquaries of London (S.A.L.), MS/872/3, *Catalogue of Plants and Seeds Which Are Sold by Conrad Loddiges* (London, 1804); *Orchideae In the Collection of Conrad Loddiges and Sons ... Organised According to Dr Lindley's Genera and Species* (London, 1839); *Stove Plants in the Collection of Conrad Loddiges and Sons* (London, 1842); *Loddiges' Palms* (London, 1845). Quoted by kind permission of the Society of Antiquaries of London.

[85] For an example of a tree catalogue, see Caldwell Archives, 1824 Tree Catalogue http://www.caldwellarchives.org.uk/plants/nursery-catalogues.html> [accessed 22 Apr. 2020].

[86] A rare example of a priced catalogue from the early 19th century was issued by William Cobbett for his American Nursery. See *Cobbett's Weekly Register*, 63 (1827), pp. 673–704.

[87] Harvey, *Early Nurserymen*, p. 65.

[88] *G.M.*, 7 (1831), p. 338.

[89] The botanist Adrian Howarth recounted a visit to James Lee's nursery where he walked in and wandered the nursery grounds without being challenged (see A. Howarth, *Observations on the Genus Mesembryanthemum* (London, 1794), p. 27).

[90] L.A., Colville Estate, IV/39/1, Ledger 1810–12. See, e.g., Mr. and Mrs. Malcolm and daughters, Feb. 1811. Purchases in person or by personal instruction can be inferred from these accounts by the absence of the customary gratuity to the gardener. The gratuity was listed as a charge to the customer, but its value was subtracted from the 'cash received' column, by which means the businessman used the customer's money to pay a commission to an intermediary. See, e.g., IV/39/5, Order Book 1834, 14 Apr.

[91] L.A., Colville Estate, IV/39/1, Ledger 1810–12; IV/39/2, Cash book 1832; IV/39/3, Cash Book Feb. 1832–Nov. 1834; IV/39/4, Roehampton cash book Aug. 1833–Oct. 1834; T.N.A., C 111, James Cochrane Day Book 1816.

[92] Colvill's ledger for 1810–12 also shows multiple transactions by Lord Galloway, Lady Bathurst, Lord and Lady Portsmouth, Lady Chesterfield, the Dowager Marchioness of Lansdown, the Countess of Northampton, Lord Torrington, the Duke of Newcastle, the Countess of Aberdeen and Lord Coventry.

[93] L.A., Colville Family Estate IV/39/5, Order book 1834.

[94] L.A., Colville Family Estate IV/39/5, Order book 1834.

[95] 1831a refers to L.A., Colville Family Estate IV/39/5, order book 1834.

[96] Chester Record Office (C.R.O.), Caldwell's Nurseries, Knutsford DDX 363/9, for all 1832 prices.

[97] 1831b refers to L.A., Colville Family Estate IV/39/7, Roehampton Nursery order book 1834.

[98] C.R.O., Caldwell's Nurseries, Knutsford DDX 363/9, for all 1830 prices.

[99] L.M.A., B/HRS/013, Samuel Harrison Letter Book 1818–19, p. 124.

[100] L.M.A., B/HRS/012, Samuel Harrison Valuation and Stock Book 1812, for 1812 prices.

[101] *Catalogue of Plants, which are sold by Conrad Loddiges & Sons, nurserymen, at Hackney, near London* (London, 1820), for all 1820 prices.

[102] C.R.O., Caldwell's Nurseries, Knutsford DDX 363/2, William Caldwell Day Book 1790–5.

[103] See S. H. Williamson and L. P. Cain, 'Defining measures of worth: most are better than the CPI' <https://www.measuringworth.com/defining_measures_of_worth.php> [accessed 12 Nov. 2018] for a discussion of the various ways in which historical worth can be assessed and the limitations of using the Consumer Price Index for historical comparisons.

[104] C. H. Feinstein, 'Pessimism perpetuated: real wages and the standard of living in Britain during and after the industrial revolution', *Journal of Economic History*, 58 (1998), pp. 625–58 (pp. 640–3).

[105] L.A., Colville Family Estate IV/39/6, Men's Time Book, Roehampton. In 1831 the weekly wage bill during much of the summer was a steady £10 10*s* 6*d*: ten staff at 13*s* 6*d* and one each at 12*s* 6*d*, 5*s*, 15*s*, £1 and £1 10*s*. Men appeared to have been paid by the hour or the half day, for payments varied from 13*s* to 14*s* 9*d* from week to week during the summer and reduced to 12*s* in the winter months for most staff.

[106] E. Baines, *History of the Cotton Manufacture in Great Britain* (London, 1835), p. 443.

[107] E. M. Boot, 'Real incomes in the British middle-class, 1760–1850: the experience of clerks at the East India Company', *Economic History Review*, 52 (1999), pp. 638–68 (p. 650).

[108] Lord Beveridge, *Prices and Wages in England from the Twelfth to the Nineteenth Century: Volume 1* (London: Frank Cass, 1965), pp. 421, 436.

[109] L.A., Colville Family Estate IV/39/5, Order Book 1834; IV/39/7, Roehampton Nursery Order Book 1834.

[110] Caldwell's Nursery was chosen as a regional comparator owing to the extensive digitization of business records of the nursery carried out by Cheshire Gardens Trust. These records are available to view at a dedicated website <http://www.caldwellarchives.org.uk> [accessed 22 Apr. 2020]. For discussion of the business, see Uings, Moth and Stevenson, *Caldwell's, Nurserymen of Knutsford*.

[111] L.M.A., B/HRS/012, Samuel Harrison Valuation and Stock Book 1812; S.A.L., MS/872/3, Conrad Loddiges Catalogue 1820.

[112] C.R.O., Caldwell's Nurseries, Knutsford DDX 363/9. The extent to which the decline in prices can be attributed to the general deflation after 1815 is unclear; changes in cultivation techniques and competition would also have influenced prices within the nursery trade.

[113] R. D. Hume, 'The value of money in eighteenth-century England: incomes, prices and buying power – and some problems in cultural economics', *Huntington Library Quarterly*, 77 (2014), pp. 373–416.

THE GARDENERS' ROYAL BENEVOLENT INSTITUTION: PRODUCT OF MUTUAL AID ASSOCIATIONS AND GARDENING NETWORKS IN THE NINETEENTH CENTURY

FRANCESCA MURRAY

ABSTRACT

The Gardeners' Royal Benevolent Institution, founded in 1839 and given the Royal accolade by Queen Victoria in 1851, came from a long heritage of fraternal activities involving gardeners. This paper examines these activities and how, as the gardening trade sought to professionalize itself and provide respectable structures of mutual aid, key practitioners and a cheap gardening press collaborated to provide a pension scheme for elderly and indigent gardeners.

INTRODUCTION

It is often said that Britain is a 'nation of gardeners' and the benefits of fresh air, creativity, and exercise mean that gardening is a popular pastime for today's pensioners who enjoy the benefits of a welfare state and occasionally a private pension. For an elderly or indigent (meaning 'poor or needy') gardener in the nineteenth century there were few silver linings in old age. Financial probity and planning for old age or illness was a respectable individual and collective demonstration of fiscal self-discipline, but it was not easy.

Today's £24.2 billion British horticultural industry originated from a transformation in the nineteenth century of the practical craft of gardening into a professional trade. Metropolitan gardeners recognised the need for a national association to provide mutual aid and fraternity. The Gardeners' Benevolent Institution (GBI) was established in 1839 and acquired its Royal status in 1851. It offered annuities to gardeners and their widows experiencing extreme hardship in old age or illness (Figure 1). It had a common heritage with earlier fraternal associations including the Worshipful Company of Gardeners, friendly and benefit societies, freemasonry and florists' societies. These will be briefly examined to demonstrate how the timing was ripe for the establishment of the GBI.

Figure 1. The Gardeners' Royal Benevolent Institution logo 1913; Hertfordshire Archives, D/ESX686/11

THE WORSHIPFUL COMPANY OF GARDENERS

One of the most ancient examples of gardeners associating as a distinct group, and a forerunner of the GBI, was the Worshipful Company of Gardeners (WCG), a minor livery company that dominated the market gardeners around the City of London until the early nineteenth century (Figure 2). First mentioned petitioning the City Corporation to be allowed to sell produce 'at the side gate of St Pauls churchyard' in 1345, the WCG received its Royal Charter in 1605 at a time when there was a strain on food supplies during the London famine.[1] It did not represent all market gardeners supplying London, but it controlled many within a six-mile radius of the City (under its 1616 Charter).[2] These gardeners supplied the City's inhabitants with a seasonal supply of food and flowers and removed human and animal excrement. The WCG offered an apprenticeship scheme, charitable giving, and freedom of the City as a mark of respectability and association. The 'ties of friendship, group commitment, loyalty'[3] were strong enough inducements to enlist members and provide fraternal and business benefits, but they were secondary to the primary aims of market controls.

The WCG relied on 'quarterage', a payment of six pence every quarter, and apprenticeship fees, but its funds were precarious at times. Its survival through the eighteenth and into the early nineteenth century demonstrates its success as a minor Guild and offers an incidental but positive example of fellowship between gardeners.[4] D.E.F. Gollin acknowledges that the WCG performed aspects of friendly society activities in the charitable expenditure on company members who had fallen on hard times, and, as a precursor of the GBI, gardener's wives or widows were treated with special respect in mutual aid terms.[5]

Figure 2. Coat of Arms granted to The Worshipful Company of Gardeners in 1905: Courtesy of the Worshipful Company of Gardeners

There was a defensiveness towards outsiders or 'higglers in plants, who impose upon the buyers rotten and decayed plants, trees and ferns without any possibility of growing'.[6] They were discouraged by the WCG rules which protected standards and prices. These restrictions revealed anti-competition sentiments towards migratory gardeners, particularly the Scots who were reputationally popular with garden owners.[7]

THE PROVISIONS OF THE GARDENERS' BENEVOLENT INSTITUTION

In the nineteenth century, London as a metropolis expanded exponentially and the WCG lost its restrictive grip on the gardening trade. It was too vast for a single City Guild to control and whilst the WCG went dormant, the Gardeners' Benevolent Institution was established in 1839 and took forward many of its associative aims. The Institution's rules were published in the gardening press, so that gardeners could understand the election process, the criteria for obtaining a pension and subscriber fees.[8] For example a gardener could apply for a pension who had 'practised gardening as a profession for subsistence for thirty years' and could supply references. Widows also had to prove the length and quality of their dead husbands' gardening employment with references. An annual subscription was one guinea, or a life subscription ten guineas, so it was a substantial part of a gardener's wages. Subscribers were initially gardening practitioners (nurserymen, head gardeners or seedsmen) and honorary amateur gardeners or wealthy (often City of London) donors. A subscription gave the gardeners access to pensions which were awarded on the basis of a poll of members. At the same time subscribers could use the votes they were allocated to ballot for financial assistance for their favoured candidate. Every subscriber received one vote but some people took out large subscriptions which gave them more votes: nurserymen, for example, might use this as a means of supporting their employees or a wealthy garden owner to finance their garden staff's retirement. Hence the ballot box was not always an honest cashier of deservingness. Although only GBI subscribers were technically allowed to receive pensions, non-subscribers could be given a pension at the discretion of the committee - and with much complaint from subscribers. Instead of a Master and Wardens, a chair and committee decided the business of the GBI and roles were populated on a strict rotation system by leading gardening practitioners.[9]

From its beginning the GBI had strong connections to the City of London; indeed it received criticism in its early years for being too London-focused. Continuing the legacy of the WCG, the City of London network became its altruistic backers and investors of its funds. The decision to invest the subscriptions in the risk averse 3 per cent consols from the start was fundamental in securing its longevity. The ongoing challenge was to ensure the friendly society was not used exclusively as a private pension scheme for its metropolitan patrons' employees.[10]

Like the WCG, the GBI held ritualized dinners and musical entertainments in various City taverns managed by stewards. A festival dinner was held annually with leading practitioners and members of the elite coming together to raise funds: the after-dinner speech by celebrity author Charles Dickens in 1852[11] provided a guilt-inducing boost to the Institution's charitable aims. The list of festival dinner presidents reads like a catalogue of the City's great and good, whilst the list of donors' names was carefully published in the gardening and national press for every gardener to see the benevolence of their masters.

BENEFIT AND FRIENDLY SOCIETIES

As urban growth and industrialization took hold, people prepared for their old age, finding schemes and support mechanisms to see them through their later years, sickness and burial. Cordery suggests that the eighteenth century saw the removal of 'paternal obligation' as a central factor for survival.[12] However, the gardening trade was slow to adapt, as a large portion of its stakeholders were intrinsically linked to past behaviours of the landed estates. In rural and semi-urban communities the parish custom of almsgiving was seen as conditional, but the publican was often an expedient credit source.[13] The early 'box' or 'benefit' clubs took the form of a locked box, often secured under the tavern bar, into which people placed spare coins. Naturally, tavern owners could be as capricious as landowners. But the box or benefit club system evolved into an informal method of collective aid and confirmed a willingness to collaborate.[14] Over time, it took on a more formal existence as part of the benefit and friendly societies which became an integral part of British working society by the nineteenth century.[15] In England there were some 9,672 friendly societies in 1802, by 1815, this number had risen to approximately 925,429 and by 1904 there were six million members of friendly societies. In metropolitan Middlesex/Surrey, where the idea of a mutual aid association for gardeners had first arisen, eight per cent of the population belonged to a friendly society by 1815.[16] Friendly societies appealed to both working and middle classes as they promoted 'self-help, independence, loyalty and a sense of community' with membership rules and ritualised practices.[17] These ideals reduced the need for state provision of poor relief. Given their level of individualism, watched over by disinterested representatives of society, as trustees and directors, the friendly societies also seemed to allay government fears of collectivism.

Two Acts of Parliament gave the membership of friendly societies their own impetus. First, the Anatomy Act of 1832[18] permitted medical teaching institutions to use the cadavers of paupers for dissection. This horrific action was seen by many as a punishment for being poor. Thus if funeral insurance was included in a friendly society's rules, its membership rose. (The GBI offered a discretionary £4 burial contribution.) The second act to have an impact was the Poor Law of 1834,[19] which ended state assistance to alleviate hardship for people living at home in the community. The institution of workhouses, especially those that were single sex and separated the aged, split families apart. The subscription to a friendly society could keep a gardener protected from this sad end.

The middle classes did not see an obligation to give their domestic employees (including their gardeners) any extra financial support unless they had shown due loyalty and deference reminiscent of the landed estate system. Asa Briggs asserted that the emerging monied citizens' awareness of their elevated 'class' created a vital distinction in how their moral and financial behaviours adjusted towards the issues of hardship and poverty.[20] A request for aid was often considered unfavourably if the individual had not had the forethought to sign up to a friendly society. The journeyman gardener who used the mobility of the market to migrate to the towns from rural employment - where the parish system of relief still existed in some form, even after the changes brought in by the Poor Act of 1834 - had only himself to rely on financially. So a subscription to a gardeners' friendly society was a prudent and respectable way to demonstrate individual fiscal responsibility, as well as providing a beneficial networking opportunity. From the point of view of its wealthy metropolitan supporters, a mutual aid scheme established by gardeners for their elderly presented little risk while offering the chance to demonstrate their altruism within a milieu – that of the newly emerging recreational activity of gardening – where the urban middle classes were emulating their behaviours. For the urban gardener himself it was a small act of protective defiance or emulation of an employer's capitalism.[21]

FREEMASONRY

The hierarchical steps of freemasonry mimic the allegorical career progression of a gardener, namely 'the apprentice' (based on Adam in the garden of Eden), 'the Journeyman' (based on Noah's ark) and the final and most prestigious 'Master Gardener' (King Solomon). By the early nineteenth century there were around 500 modern lodges and 270 ancient ones in Britain and the allegorical allusions of the Garden of Eden resonated with several gardeners.[22] However, John Loudon could account for only one London masonic gardeners' lodge - 'Adam's Lodge of London', founded on June 4, 1781.[23] One of its primary purposes was distributing employee references amongst the masonic gentry but, having only 150 members, it had dwindled away by 1827. It would take until 1893 for another gardeners' lodge to be set up. Before then, an interest in exploring the benefits offered by freemasonry was occasionally discussed in the gardening press. In 1848, an article in the *Annals of Horticulture* urged readers to consider whether 'floriculture should be like freemasonry, all who wish well to it should be joined in one common brotherhood'.[24] The eventual consecration of the Hortus Lodge in April 1893 did indeed reflect the desire within the horticultural community to embrace the practices of the masonic movement. And significantly its founding meeting was held at the offices of the GBI whose secretary, George J. Ingram, was appointed secretary of the Lodge.[25]

Parallels can be drawn between some of the rituals and allusions of freemasonry and those of the early GBI and there were similarities too in the provision of financial support but, although the friendly society movement had a reputation for secrecy and rituals, the GBI did not align itself with the clandestineness of the masons (which is surprising, as there is a wealth of evidence that gardeners can be highly secretive about certain aspects of their trade).[26] Rather, the pension ballot was held in the presence of adjudicators to ensure fair play. The publication in the gardening press of the pensioner candidate list, election results and proceedings of the festival dinner was significant for transparency, to rally subscriptions, but also to demonstrate respectability.

FLORISTS' SOCIETIES

The term 'florist' appeared in the early seventeenth century and denoted 'a person who grew plants for the sake of their decorative flowers' and 'one who grew only certain kinds of flowering plants and these to a very high standard'.[27] These included the carnation, tulip, anemone and ranunculus, selected for their beauty rather than utility. The polyanthus, pink, pansy and dahlia soon followed.[28] Florists' societies emerged as a social and business network in seventeenth-century English provincial towns and London and they regularly gathered as a distinct and vibrant community. They feasted with musical accompaniment and toasts whilst carrying out the administration of the society.[29] Often the feast's venue would be florally decorated with seasonal garlands and fruit.[30] Many of the initial GBI subscribers were metropolitan florists who followed these traditions. By the early nineteenth century floricultural shows proliferated as popular entertainment around London for both amateurs and florists selling their flowers, and vigorous networking activity ensued.[31]

George Glenny (1793-1874) was a florist, garden journalist and agitator. He was a fierce supporter of the metropolitan florists' cause which he featured enthusiastically in the first British gardening newspaper, the *Gardeners' Gazette,* which he also owned. In 1832, he established the *Metropolitan Society of Florists and Amateurs* (Figure 3). It was the most prominent of the London florists' societies, and supporters of the GBI were drawn from its ranks.[32] Meetings were held at the Crown and Anchor Tavern, close to Covent Garden market, which would also become the regular meeting place of the GBI. The creation of the Gardeners' Benevolent Institution was first mooted as an idea by Glenny in 1839 - for little motive except than that other trades had a benevolent fund. His reasoning was reported as:

> whilst the butchers, bakers, drapers and almost every other class of tradesmen, had their benevolent associations, he expressed his surprise that none had hitherto been attempted for so scientific and useful a body as the gardeners, [and] he did not know of any class who had so great a claim.[33]

Glenny's involvement with the GBI was mutually beneficial, enabling the latter to use the burgeoning gardening press as a mouthpiece in its early years, and potentially helping the former to extend his own sphere of influence. He wisely recognised the value of 'a royal flag at the mast head' for his Metropolitan Society and similarly for the GBI, whose early activities were given a boost by the royal patronage of the Duke of Cambridge.[34]

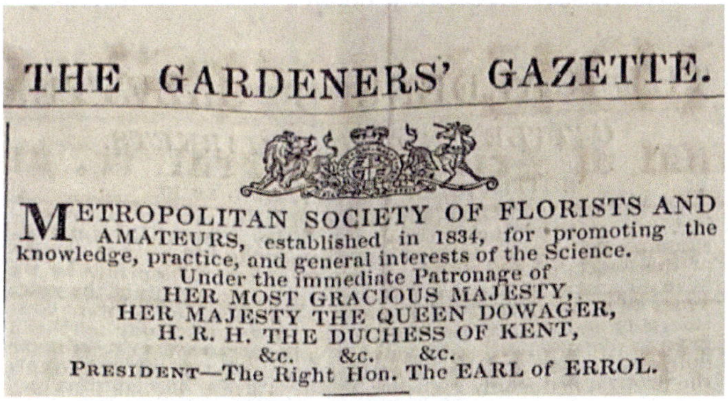

THE GARDENERS' GAZETTE.

METROPOLITAN SOCIETY OF FLORISTS AND AMATEURS, established in 1834, for promoting the knowledge, practice, and general interests of the Science.
Under the immediate Patronage of
HER MOST GRACIOUS MAJESTY,
HER MAJESTY THE QUEEN DOWAGER,
H. R. H. THE DUCHESS OF KENT,
&c. &c. &c.
PRESIDENT—The Right Hon. The EARL of ERROL.

Figure 3. Advertisement for the Metropolitan Society of Florists and Amateurs. *The Gardeners' Gazette*, 24 August 1838

Having established the *Royal Society and Central School of Horticulture* which held shows and teaching sessions, Glenny was anxious to extend the reputation of his Metropolitan Society through a national floricultural society to create the 'simple machinery' so that 'every amateur and gardener in the United Kingdom might be in communication'.[35] He could use a benevolent society as the vehicle to do this and sell more of his newspapers. However, bankruptcy, and the dominance of the elitist Horticultural Society led to Glenny's loss of influence.[36]

THE GBI'S PENSIONERS

GBI pensions of sixteen shillings for men and twelve shillings for women were 'awarded' to the most 'deserving' candidates who received the most votes from their peers. Initially, bi-annual elections were held with, as the decades passed, an ever-increasing list of candidates. The support of the *Gardeners' Chronicle*, established in 1841 and edited by John Lindley of the Horticultural Society, was hugely important for the GBI as its activities were published there for all to read. Using these records and the wider gardening press, literature, census data and historic property archives, it is possible to build a picture of the pensioners' lives and gain insights into their community. The interconnectedness of these gardeners, their relationships, the regionality and the groupings suggest both rural and urban networks. It is also possible to ascertain not just who the gardeners worked with and whether or not they moved in their career, but also where they and their families lived - elderly unemployed gardeners often lodged with younger gardeners or nephews and nieces.

The first person to be awarded a pension, in 1840, was John Standen, an estate gardener born in 1780, from Steyning in Sussex. In 1842 Sarah Attlee, wife of the late Lambeth nurseryman William Attlee, was the first widow to receive a pension. William's brother Richard, head gardener to the Beaufoys, a Quaker family of vinegar distillers in Lambeth before he set up a successful nursery in Oval, was a GBI committee member. Another widow was not so fortunate, Mary Newberry's application being rejected because her papers were not in order. The candidates for pensions suffered from rheumatism, life-limiting asthma, paralysis and broken arms from falling out of pear trees. Chiswick gardener Francis Chamberlain had a severe accident which deprived him of the use of a hand. Henry Bridden of West Kirby, a gardener all his life, walked out of a greenhouse and was stung by a bee in the eye and rendered totally blind.[37]

In 1860, when he was 72, James Wells, who had worked as a gardener since the age of 14, including for Lord Keane of Burton Lodge (now Whitehayes) near Christchurch, Hampshire, was

Figure 4. James Wells, a GBI pensioner, from *A short account of the work of the Gardeners' Royal Benevolent Institution, 1839-1903* (London: Gardeners' Royal Benevolent Institution, 1904), p. 30

allocated a pension (Figure 4). He was a GBI pensioner for thirty-one years in total, which was unusual as many died in the year of their election or shortly afterwards.[38] Unlike Wells, and more in keeping with the normal period in which gardeners held pensions, Edward Marshal, a gardener born on the Alnwick estate of the Duke of Northumberland (a GBI patron), applied for a pension thirteen times. Finally successful in 1854, he died two years later.[39]

The GBI had problems attracting regular subscribers from the trade. First, as mentioned above, subscriptions were deemed too expensive for the working gardener. Second, the elections were perceived to be engineered to benefit popular candidates who were promoted with advertisements and soft pressure. William Wells, a candidate for a pension in 1843, was supported by the nurseryman, Mr Chaundy, who solicited votes for Wells in an appeal in the *Gardeners' Chronicle*, which claimed 'there cannot be a case more deserving'. William obtained the most votes ahead of two candidates who were standing for the second time.[40] To attract more subscriptions and end the endless debate in the gardening press about 'unfair' allocations of pensions, the society changed its rules in 1860 to allow those who had been subscribers for over fifteen years to be automatically assigned a pension without election.[41]

Although there may have been some problems attracting regular subscribers, the allocation of GBI funds increased over the years. In 1908 the Gardeners' Chronicle reported that since its establishment 'a sum of nearly £122,000 has been distributed to necessitous gardeners or their widows'.[42]

CONCLUSION

A study of the GBI origins and connections highlights how it was very much a creature of the age of urbanization and industrialization, a period when mutual aid became increasingly necessary. It provided a respectable means of obtaining assistance. The institution, which had overlapping interests with other charitably oriented groups, took advantage of the burgeoning gardening press, of royal patronage, flower shows and feasts to raise both its own profile and the funds needed to support gardeners in old age and distress. It had its faults in the high cost of subscriptions relative to gardeners' pay, in an apparent bias towards metropolitan gardeners and unfairness in the allocation of pensions. Another criticism might be that the GBI, like other mutual aid associations, extended the patriarchal system of lord and master more redolent of the landed estate. It was characteristic of the nineteenth century nursery trade that head gardeners and nurserymen pursued their aims through committee membership and garden literature in emulation of their elite masters and clientele. Nevertheless, a mutual aid association that covered the vast network of practitioners of the craft helped bring them together in a semi-cohesive group, and so the GBI can be credited with giving a solid footing to what, by the end of the nineteenth century, amounted to the British horticultural industry.

REFERENCES

1 Malcolm Thick, *The Neat House Gardens: Early Market Gardening Around London* (London: Prospect Books, 1998), p. 42.

2 Thick, pp. 39-60.

3 Joan Thirsk, *Alternative Agriculture: A History from the Black Death to the Present Day* (Oxford: Oxford University Press, 2000), p.172.

4 David Marsh, 'A Fellowship on the Fringes: The Gardeners' Company of London in the Seventeenth Century' in *Guilds and Associations in Europe 900-1900,* ed. by Ian A. Gadd and Patrick Wallis (London: Centre for Metropolitan History, Institute of Historical Research, 2006), p. 128.

5 D. E. F. Gollin, *The Company Archive of the Worshipful Company of Gardeners* (privately printed for the Worshipful Company of Gardeners, 2008) p. 18.

6 Michael Leapman, *The Ingenious Mr Fairchild, The Forgotten Father of the Flower Garden* (London: Headline, 2000), p. 84.

[7] For more analysis see Ron McEwen, 'The Northern Lads: The Migration of Scottish Gardeners with Especial Reference to the Royal Botanic Gardens, Kew', *Sibbaldia: The Journal of Botanic Garden Horticulture,* 2013, pp. 109-23.
[8] *Gardeners' Chronicle*, 27 March 1841, p. 194.
[9] *Gardeners' Chronicle*, 27 March 1841, p. 194.
[10] *Gardeners' Chronicle*, 27 March 1841, p. 194.
[11] *The Speeches of Charles Dickens: A Complete Edition,* ed. by K. J. Fielding (New York; London: 1988), p. 146.
[12] Simon Cordery, *British Friendly Societies 1750-1914* (Basingstoke: Palgrave Macmillan, 2003), p. 14.
[13] Martin Gorsky, 'The Growth and Distribution of English Friendly Societies in the early Nineteenth Century', *The Economic History Review*, New Series, 51.3 (August 1998), pp. 489-511 (p. 506).
[14] Gorsky, p. 506.
[15] Helen Merrell Lynd, *England in the Eighteen Eighties: Toward a Social Basis for Freedom* (London: Frank Cass, 1945) p. 245.
[16] Simon Cordery, 'Friendly Societies and the Discourse of Respectability in Britain, 1825-1875', *Journal of British Studies,* 34.1 (January 1995), pp. 35-48.
[17] Daniel Weinbren, 'Supporting Self Help, Charity, Mutuality, and Reciprocity in Nineteenth-Century Britain' in *Charity and Mutual Aid in Europe and North America since 1800*, ed. by Bernard Harris and Paul Bridgen (New York: Routledge, 2007), p. 68.
[18] Anatomy Act, 1832 (2 & 3 William IV, c.75).
[19] Poor Law Amendment Act, 1834 (4 & 5 William IV, c. 76).
[20] Asa Briggs, *The Age of Improvement, 1783-1867* (London: Longman 1959), p. 65.
[21]H.M. Lynd gives an insight into the working man who by investing his capital became 'a diminutive capitalist with his 'shares' and his accumulated equity', see p. 244.
[22]Arnold Steele, *The Worshipful Company of Gardeners of London: A History of its Revival 1890-1960* (London: Worshipful Company of Gardeners, 1964), p.17.
[23] John Claudius Loudon, An *Encyclopaedia of Gardening: Comprising the Theory and Practice of Horticulture, Floriculture, Arboriculture, and Landscape-gardening* (London: Longman, Rees, Orme, Brown and Green, 1827), p. 1132.
[24] *Annals of Horticulture; and Year-book of Information on Practical Gardening* for1848, pp. 498-9.
[25] Museum of Freemasonry, Hortus Lodge No 2469 meeting pamphlet, LF2469.
[26] Richard Andrew Berman, *The Architects of Eighteenth-Century English Freemasonry, 1720 – 1740*, doctoral thesis, University of Exeter, 2010, p. 286.
[27] Ruth Duthie, *Florists Flowers and Societies* (Princes Risborough: Shire Publications, 1988), p. 5.
[28] Catherine Horwood, *Potted History: The Story of Plants in the Home* (London: Francis Lincoln, 2007), p. 47.
[29] Brent Elliott, 'Flower Shows in Nineteenth-Century England', *Garden History* 29:2 (2001), pp. 171 – 84.
[30] John Harvey, *Early Nurserymen* (London: Phillimore, 1974), p. 4.
[31] *West Kent Guardian,* 1 October 1836.
[32] Loudon, p. 1240.
[33] *Gardeners' Gazette*, 19 January 1839, pp. 42-3.
[34] *Morning Herald,* 25 May 1836, p. 3. Unlike the florists, the GBI did not hold floral competitions as part of its programme but two early fundraising shows attended by the duke were held at the White Hart Hotel, Bromley, owned by an enterprising publican and florist, William Pawley – *Gardeners' Chronicle*, 14 June 1845, p. 402; *United Gardeners' and Land Stewards' Journal*, 14 June 1845, p. 380.
[35] 'Proposed Horticultural Reunion', in *Glenny's Quarterly Review of Horticulture, Literature, the Arts and General Science* (London: G. Cox, 1853), pp. 118-21.
[36] On the Horticultural Society see Brent Elliott, *The Royal Horticultural Society: A History 1804-2004* (Chichester: Phillimore, 2004).
[37]Gardeners' Benevolent Fund Minutes, 5 May 1840, and *A short account of the work of the Gardeners' Royal Benevolent Institution,* 1939-1903 (London: Gardeners' Royal Benevolent Institution, 1904), p. 47.
[38] *A short account of the work of the Gardeners' Royal Benevolent Institution,* p. 30.
[39] *Gardeners' Chronicle,* 21 January, 1854, p.33.
[40] *Gardeners' Chronicle*, 20 May 1843, p. 329; *Gardeners' Chronicle,* 3 June 1843, p.369.
[41] Minutes of Gardeners' Royal Benevolent Fund AGM 1850, no page number.
[42] *Gardeners' Chronicle*, 4 July 1908.

2

NEW PERSPECTIVES ON THE SEVENTEENTH CENTURY

If the seventeenth century was marked by political and religious turmoil in Britain, there were upheavals too in attitudes towards the natural world. Propelled by factors such as the opening up to imports from distant lands and Protestant reformation, the new natural philosophy, championed in the early part of the century by Francis Bacon, focused on shedding Aristotelian beliefs in favour of observation and experimentation.

However, a study of the pages of some early and mid-century books relating to gardens reveals that the shift in attitudes was far from sudden or dramatic. The first paper in this chapter draws on a variety of printed works from the earlier part of the seventeenth century and reflects on how strongly people connected themselves with the plant world. The second paper focuses on just two books which dealt with bees and the hives that were to be found in many gardens. Demonstrating anthropocentric attitudes like the first, it considers how bees and their behaviour were thought to provide a new understanding of people and nature and to offer pointers towards moral, ethical and political, improvement. However, where the study on bees varies from that on plants is in indicating that there was a greater inclination to interrogate nature through first hand observation and testing. Although some might have argued that meddling with nature was sacrilege, for others it was almost a duty. Henry Power voiced this view in 1660, writing that 'this World was made not onely to be inhabited, but Studied and Contemplated by Man [...] 'tis a Tribute we ought to pay him [God] for being men'.[1] The physico-theology mentioned in the second paper was similarly based on the theory that scientific investigation was a way to learn more about God's plan for humanity.

[1] Henry Power, *Experimental Philosophy* (London: John Martin and James Allestry, 1661), p. 183.

'WE ARE BUT FLOWERS THAT GLIDE': BELIEFS ABOUT PLANTS AND PEOPLE IN THE EARLY-SEVENTEENTH CENTURY

KATHERINE MYERS

ABSTRACT

To understand the horticulture of the first half of the seventeenth century, we need to consider the intellectual context within which plants and gardens were studied at the time, and to become aware of thought processes and beliefs different from our own. The cosmos was conceived as possessing a high degree of consistency between its constituent parts, providentially bestowed by God. This meant that the human and plant worlds could be regarded as closely related, materially, dynamically, and morally, and understood through the overlapping logics of analogy, causation, and the application of ethical and religious norms.

INTRODUCTION

When we investigate gardens of the past and their plants, we do not often think about what these meant to the people concerned, or the assumptions they made. Nor do we ask whether their ways of thinking might have been different from ours. If, however, we pay attention to clues scattered in introductions and title-pages to gardening books, or more widely in the literature of the time, we may be surprised by what we find.

I would like to consider in this context the first half of the seventeenth century, when the so-called scientific revolution was beginning to get under way, but many older ideas, often originating in antiquity, persisted. What is striking is how closely different aspects of the natural world were thought to be inter-related: it was believed that nature was always self-consistent, so what pertained in one area was likely to prevail in another. For example, the heavenly bodies were seen to move in circles, so circularity was thought to be embedded in the way nature operated (plants, for example, have roughly circular stems).[1] William Harvey (1578—1657), confirming in 1628 that blood circulates, pointed out that Aristotle had likened the circulation of water on earth and in the air to the orbits of the heavenly bodies.[2] Later, on the basis of Harvey's brilliant discovery, others further suggested (wrongly) that sap must circulate in plants. The debate continued into the eighteenth century.[3]

As demonstrated by Robert Fludd's *Integrae naturae speculum, artisque imago* (Figure 1) it was assumed that knowledge of plants would help the understanding of people and vice-versa. I would like to look at three overlapping mechanisms by which they were felt to illuminate each other: firstly by analogy, as we have seen with the question of circulation; secondly through cause and effect; and thirdly through ethical and religious norms, which were believed to operate as much in the natural as in the human world. The sources were twofold: classical philosophy, particularly Aristotle's, which (though it was beginning to be questioned) had dominated thinking since the Middle Ages; and the Bible, which was regarded as the vehicle of literal and incontrovertible truth.

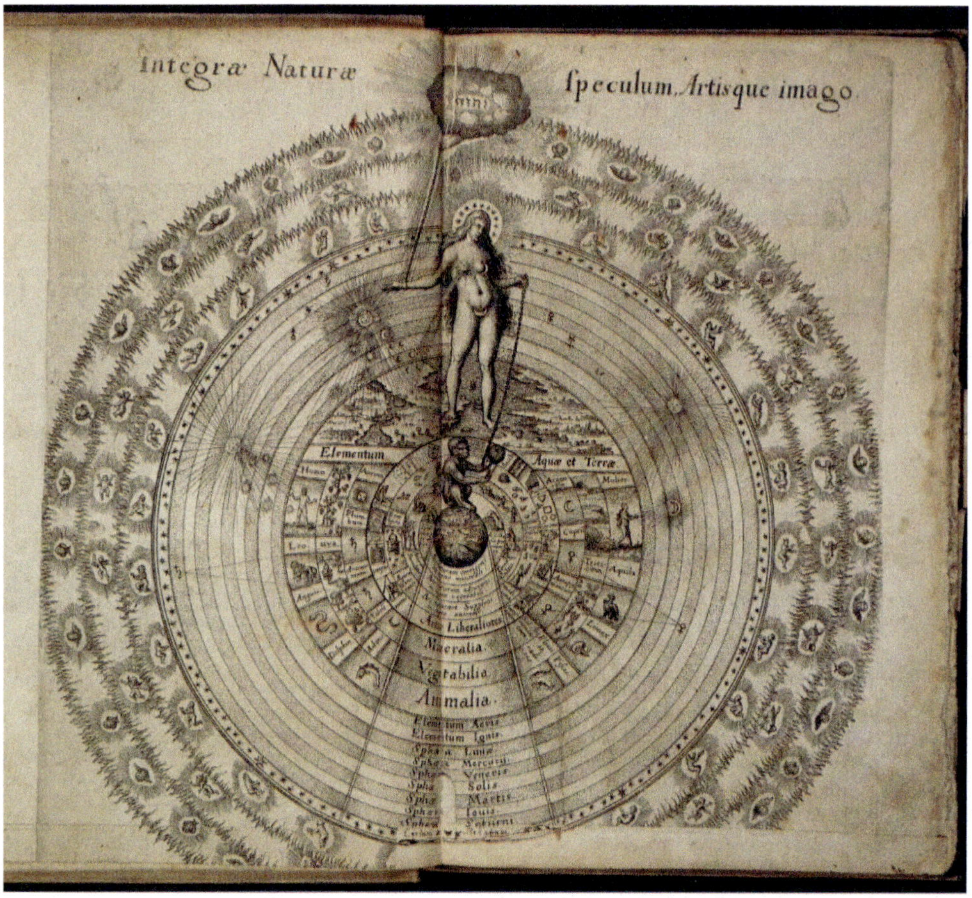

Figure 1. Robert Fludd, *Integrae naturae speculum, artisque imago* ('The Mirror of the whole of nature and the image of art'), 1617—1618. Wellcome Collection, CCA 4.0

Analogy

Analogical thinking was pervasive at this period. It went further than metaphor: in fact it was often thought of as a kind of proof of a proposition. What happened in one area could confirm what was speculated about another in similar circumstances.

Spring

The doctrine of the resurrection of the body was problematic, but it was backed up by a horticultural parallel which was cited in scripture: a seed planted in autumn would rot in the ground over winter, but only if it 'died' in this way could it subsequently burst into life.[4] For John Evelyn (1620—1706) the coming of spring to the garden was 'a kind of Resurrection of the dead, & the noblest argument of its veracity'.[5] Similarly, the traditional pre-Harvey view of sap was that it rose in spring but fell back into the roots in winter, and this was mirrored in feelings about youth or age and death in humans. In his Sonnet 15 William Shakespeare (1564—1616) contemplates young men 'Vaunt in their youthful sap' being brought to decay by time.[6] John Donne (1572—1631), mourning at midnight on the shortest day of the year a loved woman's death, imagines 'the world's whole sap' or 'general balm', which was thought to keep plants alive, as having sunk into the 'hydroptic earth', and likens this process to life gradually leaving a human body, shrinking 'as to the bed's-feet'. But the comparison is not complete: Donne contemplates the fact that whereas in nature life will revive in spring, for humanity the only return after death will be in 'the next world', for which he must prepare himself.[7]

Before sin and death entered the world there had been both eternal youth and perpetual spring, supposedly present in both the mythical Golden Age of classical antiquity and the biblical Garden of Eden. Attempts were made to re-create at least in gardens a year-round spring : in 1597 John Gerard (c.1545—1612), gardener to Lord Burghley, for example, claimed to produce 'a flourishing shew of Summer beauties in the midst of Winters force, and a goodly spring of flours, when abroad a leafe is not to be seene'.[8] A blueprint for this was set out by Francis Bacon (1561—1626) in his essay 'Of Gardens' (1625), in which he suggested that it would be possible to maintain a continuous succession of flowering plants throughout the year, thus achieving a *ver perpetuum*.[9]

Families

Another area of analogy between human and plant life was family relationships, although nothing was known in the earlier 1600s about the facts of sexual reproduction in plants, which only began to be appreciated in the closing years of the century. Male and female plants of the same species were sometimes distinguished, but only in varieties with slightly differing characteristics which could be ascribed to gender, such as size and vigour, which Bacon referred to as a 'Binarium' of stronger and weaker 'in all living bodies'.[10] Peonies, for example, came in two main types differing slightly in details of the leaves and roots, making them analogous to brothers and sisters in a human family. There was, however, a third type, which when planted resembled the male form, but when dug up its roots revealed it to be feminine. Gerard excoriated it as 'Bastarde, Misbegotten, of neither or both, but as it were a plant participating of the male and female'.[11] It could therefore be classed as a 'monster', illegitimate because it departed from the species-types named by Adam in the Garden of Eden. Nevertheless, some 'bastard' varieties were much prized because they looked spectacular, as for example John Tradescant's multi-petalled 'great Rose Daffodill', in 1629 proclaimed by John Parkinson (1567—1650) to be 'the greatest double yellow bastard Daffodill', and the 'Prince of Daffodills'.[12]

On the other hand, there was one plant association which could be framed psychologically as a type of marriage. From classical times pruned elms had been used in Italy to support vines, and the tree became the emblem of the strong faithful husband protecting the weak and dependant (but fruitful) wife, even in a country where the horticultural practice was unknown.[13] Palm-trees too were supposed to be gendered, the males and females portrayed as bending towards each other amorously.[14] But the cosmic coupling which underlay all plant procreation was that of the sun and earth. In 1617 William Lawson (1554—1635) maintained that 'Most seedes [. . .] are renued, their mother the earth keeping them in her bowels, till the Sunne their Father can reach them with his heate', warmth and moisture being prerequisites for the creation of life.[15]

Cause and Effect

In the early-seventeenth century human life presented many effects for which the causes were unknown, particularly in the areas of health and sickness, life and death. Why, for example, did people appear to die simply of old age, or could on occasion be brought back from seeming death? On the other hand, some plants exhibited surprising characteristics which had no immediately identifiable purpose. What effects might they in fact have? These questions invited speculation, and some had done so for centuries.

Stars

The medical world of the early-seventeenth century largely derived from that established by Galen, a Greek physician of the second and third centuries AD. It was assumed that everything in the sub-lunar world consisted of four elements, earth, air, fire and water, and was affected by the sun, moon, planets and 'fixed stars'. 'This huge stage presenteth naught but shows/ Whereon the stars in secret influence comment', wrote Shakespeare in Sonnet 15. As a result 'Men as plants increase', / Cheerèd and checked by the selfsame sky'.[16]

According to Galen, human health was the result of a harmonious balance in the body of the elements, each of which displayed two of four possible qualities: hot, cold, wet and dry: fire was hot and dry; air hot and wet; water cold and wet; and earth cold and dry. As plants had the same constituents, any imbalance could be righted by a remedy containing the missing qualities. Why, however, were particular plants hot or cold, moist or astringent in the first place? The stars could supply the answer: Nicholas Culpeper (1616—1654) thought that only 'artists in Astrology [. . .] are fit to make Physitions', and in his herbal (1652) he was able to inform the reader which planet governed which plant.[17] (We are still in the Ptolemaic universe in this context, so 'planets' included the sun and moon.) They had their own characteristics: Culpeper explained that Mars and Venus, for example, were opposites in all respects, Mars being hot and dry, and Venus cool and wet, among other differences.[18]

The constellations of fixed stars which rose above the horizon in the order of the Zodiac also had effects. Saffron, according to Culpeper, was 'an herb of the *Sun*, and under *the Lion* (Leo), and therefore you need not demand a reason why it strengthens the heart so exceedingly'.[19] Analogy was at work here: the sun was the ruler of the heavens, the lion the king of beasts, and the heart the most important organ in the body, so of course saffron would benefit the heart. But crucially, it was assumed that people were governed by the stars in the same ways and for the same reasons as plants, which explained why plant remedies could be effective.

In his 'Address to the Reader' Culpeper justifies his reasoning, moving from cause to effect and then back again:

> I knew well enough the whole world and everything in it was formed of a Composition of contrary Elements, and in such a harmony as must needs show the wisdom and Power of a great God. I knew as well this Creation though thus composed of contraries was one united Body, and man an Epitome of it, I knew those various affections in man in respect of Sickness and Health were caused Naturally [. . .] by the various operations of the *Macrocosm* [the entire cosmos]; and I could not be ignorant, that as the Cause is, so must the Cure be, and therefore he that would know the Reason of the operation of Herbs must look up as high as the Stars, and this is enough one would think to teach a man by the Effect where the Cause lay.[20]

The qualities apparent in plants and stars were also to be found in the four humours that controlled human bodies and minds: blood, phlegm, bile and black bile. Blood (hot and wet) produced the sanguine temperament; phlegm (cold and wet) the phlegmatic; bile (hot and dry) the choleric; and black bile (cold and dry) the melancholic. These had to be 'tempered' so that they balanced each other, any disproportion being countered either by an opposite plant to reduce a superfluity, or a similar one to remedy a lack. This was expressed in terms of human feeling: 'sympathy and antipathy are the Hinges upon which the whol [*sic*] Moddel of Physick turns', wrote Culpeper.[21] While he believed saffron strengthens the heart, he also thought it 'purges Phlegm'.[22] Though having a physical basis, the 'temperaments' were psychological, and plant remedies could have psychological effects: borage and bugloss, for example, expelled 'Pensiveness and Melancholy', the result of too much black bile. Plant remedies addressed the whole person.[23]

Spirit

Paracelsus (Philippus Aureolus Theophrastus Bombastus von Hohenheim, 1493—1541), a Swiss doctor and alchemist, had also believed in the importance of the stars in medicine, and turned his attention to the mechanism by which they influenced life on earth, for good and ill. This was through their emission of a kind of vapour, known as 'spirit', from Latin *spiritus*, meaning 'breath', which was absorbed by everything below.[24] From classical times it was believed that this contained a force that moulded the forms of inorganic matter, preserving them from disintegration, and powered life, growth and change in all living things. It was conceived as a highly attenuated and invisible form of matter, hovering between the material and mental worlds, in man linking body and soul: breathed in and absorbed by the blood it powered the heart as 'vital spirit' and was then transferred to the brain, becoming 'animal spirit', from *anima*, soul. As Donne wrote:

> our blood labours to beget
> Spirits, as like souls as it can,
> Because such fingers need to knit
> That subtle knot, that makes us man.[25]

According to Bacon's *History of Life and Death* (1623), spirit, composed of air and fire, was always trying to convert the moisture of the human body into more spirit, thus drying and weakening it, which allowed the vital spirit to escape and led to death in old age.[26]

Plants, too, were said to absorb spirit, enabling them to grow, flower, and produce seeds. Culpeper believed there was 'a Vital Spirit in every Seed to beget its like'.[27] Vegetable spirit, moreover, displayed the active characteristics of its particular plant, which could be isolated by distillation, the chief method by which plant medicines were produced. Alchemists were even attempting by multiple distillations to create an elixir that might bring back the dead; Paracelsus believed one would enable everyone to live as long as Adam.[28] Cerimon in Shakespeare's *Pericles* restores Queen Thaisa to life through his 'secret art' and 'the blest infusions /That dwells [*sic*] in vegetives, in metals, stones'. He claims that 'Death may usurp on nature many hours, /And yet the fire of life kindle again /The o'erpressed spirits.'[29] Spirit, therefore, was assumed to be the cause of many otherwise unexplained processes, but because it was defined as an invisible and subtle substance its presence was impossible to verify by experiment.

Figure 2. Pierre Pena and Matthias de l'Obel, *Stirpium adversaria nova* ('A new compendium of plants'), 1570, title-page. The man on the right is distilling with an alembic to isolate the spirits rained down by the heavenly bodies. Wellcome Library, CCA 4.0

Signatures

Another pervasive theory was the doctrine of plant signatures, but in that case it was the effect rather than the cause that was to be discovered. It had been noticed from classical times that some features of plants seemed to resemble the part of the body they were used to cure, and this came to be regarded by Paracelsus and his followers as a causal link: as William Coles (1626—62) put it in his herbal *Adam in Eden* (1657): 'The Signatures [. . .] being as it were the Books out of which the Ancients first learnt the Vertues of Herbes; Nature or rather the God of nature, having stamped on divers of them legible Characters to discover their uses.'[30] The cause, then, of the plant's healing power was God's creative will, and its appearance a hint to mankind as to what it should be used for, employing analogical thinking. The most striking example was the walnut, which Coles thought had 'the perfect Signature of the Head'. The green outer covering resembled the scalp and hair, and so was good for wounds to the head; the shell was like the skull, and the nut or kernel itself had 'the very figure of the brain'. If the kernel was mashed, moistened with 'the quintessence of Wine' and laid on the crown, it would 'comfort the brain and head mightily'.[31]

Ethical and Religious Norms

Paradise

It will already be clear that the study of plants and gardens at this period could not be isolated from a moral and doctrinal context. It was not accidental, for example, that Coles's herbal, which had practical medicinal aims, was called *Adam in Eden*. Eden was the place where nature and human nature had existed in perfection, before both fell from that state of grace. Not only was Adam required to dress and keep the garden, but he was imbued by God with knowledge of plants and their properties, which was not altogether lost after the Fall. It was thought that this was transmitted down the generations to Solomon, who knew all plants, 'from the cedar tree that is in Lebanon even unto the hyssop that springeth out of the wall', and was presumed to have written a lost treatise on botany.[32] Plantin of Antwerp, at the time the leading publisher of scientific books, used the same magnificent title page for a botanical work by Charles de l'Ecluse (1526—1609 - Clusius) and a slightly later one by Rembert Dodoens (1516 or 1517—1585 - Dodoneus): at the top is the Hebrew name of God with beneath, on the left, Adam, the practical gardener holding a plant and, on the right, Solomon with his book. At the bottom are Theophrastus and Dioscorides, the ancient authorities on theoretical and medical botany respectively (Figure 3). This arrangement represented the channel by which knowledge was transmitted to the current author from God.[33] In England on the title-page of Parkinson's florilegium *Paradisi in sole paradisus terrestris* (1629) was the Hebrew name of God again, below which was an image of the Garden of Eden, with Adam and Eve tending the different species.[34]

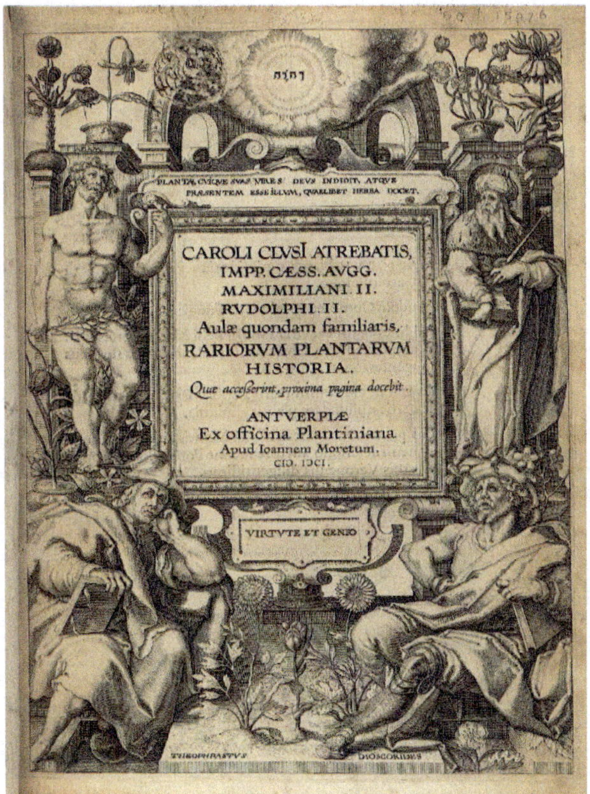

Figure 3. Title page of Charles de l'Ecluse's *Rariorum plantarum historia* (An account of rare plants, 1601). Wellcome Library, CCA 4.0

Art and Nature

Nature was implicated with humanity in the Fall. 'Both beasts and plants', wrote Donne, 'cursed in the curse of man. /So did the world from the first hour decay'.[35] Perpetual spring gave way to the four seasons, and the earth spontaneously produced thorns and thistles. Henceforth hard work would be needed just to gain a subsistence. Many, however, believed there was a way back to Eden, both morally and horticulturally: as Evelyn put it (later in the seventeenth century), Adam and his descendants 'began, with the indulgence of heaven, to recover that by Arte and Industrie, which was before produced to them Spontaneously; and to improve the Fruites of the Earth'.[36] This would entail, however, nature giving way to art in order 'to bring the earth and its inhabitants back to a pristine state of grace'.[37]

This view prevailed over the first half of the seventeenth century, as Charles Webster has shown, although there were some who demurred.[38] Nature as creation might have fallen, but nature as creator still executed the divine will, and it could be considered sacrilege to suggest that it might be improved by human art. Shakespeare dramatized the argument in a crucial scene in *The Winter's Tale* (1610—11), in which the shepherdess Perdita refuses to plant striped carnations in her garden, calling them 'bastards', because 'there is an art which in their piedness shares /With great creating nature'.[39] The art in question was propagation from cuttings rather than seed. A chance variation could produce stripes, but to be sure of maintaining them in the next generation the plant would have to be cloned. It was seed, however, that was 'the natural way of plants' and the divinely ordained method of propagation, according to Thomas Browne (1605—82), who in 1646 quoted Genesis: 'Let the earth bring forth grasse, and herbe yeelding seed, and the tree yeelding fruit, whose seed is in it selfe.'[40] Against this view Perdita's interlocutor Polixenes argues that art can only improve nature by using nature's methods. He gives the example of grafting and budding to meliorate the quality of fruit, claiming that 'The art itself is nature'.[41] The poet Andrew Marvell (1621--78) later disagreed: he rejected these techniques because they produced 'forbidden mixtures' and 'uncertain and adulterate fruit': 'no plant now knew the stock from which it came', so they were both transgressive and morally impure.[42]

In the 1650s, however, some people were interpreting both nature and grafting in a contrary sense. Ralph Austen (1612—76) was both an expert fruit grower and an ardent Calvinist, as well as the author of a book (1653) in which each of the two aspects of his life is examined in the light of the other. The first half, *A Treatise of Fruit-Trees*, is a horticultural handbook, while the second, *The Spiritual Use of an Orchard,* interprets the relevant gardening techniques in terms of Calvinist doctrine. At the beginning of the first part Austen considers Adam's role in Eden, which was 'to keepe and order the Garden of Fruit-trees' planted by God himself. In the second part, however, he shows how after the Fall just as 'the Husbandman makes choice of what wild plants he pleaseth, to bring into his Orchards, there to Graft, and order to fruit-bearing from yeare to yeare', so 'God [. . .] chose some wild plants [. . .]to plant in his Orchard, [. . .] and let others alone to grow wild, and bring forth their natural fruit', but as this is 'sower, bitter and poysonous', these trees 'are not brought into his Church, nor ingrafted into Christ'.[43] Plant selection and grafting were thus translated into the Calvinist doctrine of salvation only for God's elect, and 'nature' became the unregenerate condition of lost souls or wild trees.

The first half of the seventeenth century was a period of political and religious strife, an unlikely time to find a pervasive belief in a coherent and harmonious cosmos in which humanity had a central place.

But Anglicans and Calvinists, Royalists and Parliamentarians, although they may have differed over the arrangement of the pieces, must all have taken heart from the thought that they were part of a divinely controlled order. For gardeners, reflections between the human and horticultural worlds would have bolstered that reassurance.

REFERENCES

[1] See *The Garden of Cyrus*, in *Sir Thomas Browne: The Major Works*, ed. by C. A. Patrides (London: Penguin Books, 1977), pp. 318—388 (p. 372).
[2] William Harvey, *An Anatomical Disquisition on the Motion of the Heart*, trans. by Robert Willis (London and New York: J. M. Dent, 1906), p. 5.
[3] See Stephen Switzer, *The Nobleman, Gentleman, and Gardener's Recreation* (London: B. Barker and C. King, 1715), pp. 121-3.
[4] *The Holy Bible*, Authorized Version, John, 12.24; also Corinthians, 15, 35—8.
[5] John Evelyn, *Elysium Britannicum, or the Royal Gardens*, ed. by John Ingram (Philadelphia: University of Pennsylvania Press, 2001), p. 335.
[6] William Shakespeare, *Sonnets and a Lover's Complaint*, Sonnet 15, l. 7 (first published in 1609), in *The Complete Works*, ed. by Stanley Wells and Gary Taylor (Oxford: Clarendon Press, 1988), pp. 749—775 (p. 752).
[7] John Donne, 'A Nocturnal upon S. Lucy's Day, being the shortest day', first published in 1633, *The Complete English Poems*, ed. by A. J. Smith (London: Penguin Books, 1971), pp. 72—3.
[8] John Gerard, *The Herball or Generall Historie of Plantes* (London: John Norton, 1597), no page number.
[9] Francis Bacon, 'Of Gardens', in *The Essayes or Counsels* (1625), *The Oxford Francis Bacon*, vol. XV, ed. by Michael Kiernan (Oxford: Clarendon Press, 1985),139-45 (pp. 139, 139-40).
[10] Francis Bacon, *Sylva Sylvarum, or, A Natural History in ten Centuries* (London: W. Rawley, 1627), VII, 155.
[11] Gerard, *Herball*, p. 830.
[12] John Parkinson, *Paradisi in sole paradisus terrestris* (London: H. Lowndes and R. Young, 1629), p. 102.
[13] Shakespeare, *Comedy of Errors,* XII. 2. 177—9, *Complete Works*, p. 264.
[14] Josuah Sylvester, *The Divine Weeks and Works*, [. .] *mostly translated from the French of William de Saluste, Lord of the Bartas* (first published in 1605), ed. by Theron Wilbur Haight (Waukesha, Wis., USA: H. M. Youmans, 1908), p. 178.
[15] William Lawson, *The Countrie Housewifes Garden* (London: Roger Jackson, 1617), p. 18.
[16] Shakespeare, Sonnet 15, ll 3—4, 5—6, *Complete Works*, p. 752.
[17] Nicholas Culpeper, *The English Physitian*, (London: Peter Cole, 1652), p. 244.
[18] Ibid., p. 239.
[19] Ibid., p. 212.
[20] Ibid, 'To the Reader'.
[21] Ibid., p. 44.
[22] Ibid., p. 212.
[23] Ibid., p.18.
[24] See Philip Ball, *The Devil's Doctor* (London: Arrow Books, 2007), pp. 246—7.
[25] John Donne, 'The Extasy', ll. 61—4, first published in 1733, *Complete English Poems*, pp. 53—5 (p. 55).
[26] Francis Bacon, *The History of Life and Death* (London: Humphrey Mosley, 1638), pp. 282—323.
[27] Culpeper, p. 238.
[28] *The Hermetic and Alchemical Writings of* [. . .] *Paracelsus*, trans. and ed. by Arthur Edward Waite, 2 vols (London: James Elliott, 1894), II, 69—70.
[29] Shakespeare, *Pericles, Prince of Tyre*, XII.32—3, 80—2, *Complete Works*, pp.1053—4.
[30] William Coles, 'Further Account of work', *Adam in Eden: or, Natures Paradise* (London: J. Streater , 1657), no page numbers. The idea that the purpose of something was a kind of cause derived from Aristotle's category of 'final' causes.
[31] Ibid., p. 3.
[32] *Bible*, I Kings 4:33.

[33] Charles de l'Ecluse, *Rariorum plantarum historia* (Antwerp: Plantin, 1601), frontispiece; Rembert Dodoens, *Historia plantarum pemptades sex* (Antwerp: Plantin, 1616), frontispiece.
[34] Parkinson, *Paradisus terrestris* , frontispiece.
[35] Donne, 'An Anatomy of the World: The First Anniversary', ll. 200—1, first published in 1633, *The Complete English Poems*, pp. 269-83 (p. 275).
[36] Evelyn, p. 29.
[37] Jim Bennett and Scott Mandelbrote, *The Garden, the Ark, the Tower and the Temple* (Oxford: Museum of the History of Science with the Bodleian Library, 1998), p. 8.
[38] Charles Webster, *The Great Instauration*: *Science, Medicine and Reform 1626—1660* (London: Duckworth, 1975).
[39] Shakespeare, *The Winter's Tale*, IV.4. 87—8, *Complete Works*, p. 1118.
[40] *Sir Thomas Browne's Pseudodoxia Epidemica* (first published in 1646), ed. by Robin Robbins, 2 vols (Oxford: Clarendon Press, 1981), I, 206.
[41] Shakespeare, *The Winter's Tale*, IV.4. 97, *Complete Works*, p. 1118.
[42] Andrew Marvell, 'The Mower against gardens', ll. 20—25 (first published in 1681), in *Andrew Marvell*, ed. by Frank Kermode and Keith Walker (Oxford and New York: Oxford University Press, 1990), pp. 40—1 (p. 40).
[43] Ralph Austen, *A Treatise of Fruit-Trees* and *The Spiritual Use of an Orchard, or Garden*, second edition (Oxford: Thomas Robinson, 1657), p. 12; pp. 1, 2.

A DIVINE SOCIETY:
BEEKEEPING, OBSERVATION AND POLITICAL SCIENCE IN SEVENTEENTH-CENTURY ENGLAND

MARLIS HINCKLEY

ABSTRACT

Amidst the political turmoil of the seventeenth century, English writers turned to bees – long recognized for their complex social organization – as examples of the perfect society. Certain of these writings, such as the works of clergyman Samuel Purchas and royal beekeeper Moses Rusden, combined the direct observation of bees with moralizing writing about their significance as examples of good governance. In doing so, they united a new interest in observation as an epistemological technique with an older, Christian vision of nature, presenting scientific investigation as a way to learn more about God's plan for humanity.

INTRODUCTION

Bees, according to Aristotle, are political animals.[1] The classical philosopher, pointing to their seamless cooperation and apparent social stratification, was one of the many early writers to understand bee society through the lens of its human counterpart. Bees – specifically, honeybees, one of the world's few domesticated insects – provided potent terms for describing human society not only because of their social organization, but also because of their familiarity. Hives were a regular feature in gardens across Europe, making them among the continent's most familiar and best-loved insects.[2]

In the early modern period, parallels between bee society and its human counterpart allowed writers to both discuss bees using human terms and humans using bee terms. Works like Phillips van Marnix's *Beehive of the Romish Church* (1569) or Bernard Mandeville's famous *Fable of the Bees* (1705) satirized and critiqued human societies using the allegory of a beehive. At the same time, horticultural literature like Charles Butler's *The Feminine Monarchie* (1609) used contemporary political developments to characterize and understand the behaviour of bees.[3] Certain works combined elements of both lines of thought, suggesting that bee society might be an allegory for its human counterpart in more than just a literary sense. Pedro Mexio's *Treasurie of Auncient and Moderne Times*, translated into English in 1613, held that 'the form of a Commonwealth observed amongst Bees, methinks is so proper and answerable unto that of men: as it may be verily presumed, that God gave them it by a Natural instinct, and for an instruction unto our manner of Government.'[4] Baldassare Castiglione's *Book of the Courtier*, translated into English in 1588, raised bee society as an example in its discussion of whether monarchy or republicanism was 'more accordant with nature'.[5] Drawing on a Medieval Christian tradition of seeing nature as a source of signs for humankind, these writers suggested that by observing bees, humans could potentially access truths about proper governance inaccessible in other ways.

Amidst the political turmoil of seventeenth-century England, the question of proper governance was an urgent one. Bees were frequently connected with this topic, appearing as representatives of government in works from Thomas Hobbes' *Leviathan* (1651) to John Milton's *Paradise Lost* (1667).[6] At times, this allegorical bee writing overlapped with the growing genre of beekeeping literature, as in the compilation of a diverse range of letters which formed Samuel Hartlib's *Reformed Commonwealth of Bees* (1655). As natural and political creatures, bees occupied a special, intermediate place in the early modern world, living in a society analogous to that of humans while also forming part of the divinely-ordained natural order.[7] Consequently, for some early modern thinkers, the study of bees could provide a way to study the divine plan.

This chapter will examine two particular English books about bees from the seventeenth century: Samuel Purchas's *A Theatre of Politicall Flying-Insects*, printed in 1657, and Moses Rusden's *A Further Discovery of Bees*, published some twenty years later. The former, published under the Protectorate, used the language of observation to paint a picture of a communitarian bee state, putting forward a blueprint for a 'physico-theology' that would study nature in order to draw conclusions about the ideal state of society. The latter, written during the reign of Charles II, took a very similar approach, but drew conclusions that re-emphasized the importance of the hereditary monarchy. These texts united the centuries-old tradition of seeing bees as a metaphor for human society with a new interest in eyewitness observation, bringing the two together in service of a reforming project capable of re-imagining a new form of society better aligned with the divine plan. As such, they represented a profound shift in the relationship between theology and observational science, bringing the two into an alignment in which garden beehives could serve as a source of moral insight.

PURCHAS AND THE *THEATRE OF POLITICALL FLYING-INSECTS*

Samuel Purchas's *Theatre of Politicall Flying-Insects* provides an encyclopaedic account of the anatomy, social structure, generation, diets, habits, management and products of bees, discussing everything from 'the Excellency of Bees' to the 'Seats for the Hives, and Bee-Garden.[8] Some two hundred pages in length, the work draws on over three hundred named authorities, from classical authors like Pliny and Aristotle to near-contemporaries like Richard Remnant and John Levett (Figure 1).

Little is known about Purchas; though he shared his name with his better-known father, the author of the travelogues entitled *Purchas, his Pilgrimage* (1613), the *Theatre* is the only known work of the younger Purchas. According to Harry B. Weiss, he was likely born around the turn of the seventeenth century. Educated at Cambridge, he became a minister, and was employed as the rector of Sutton, Essex until his death around 1658.[9] He is known to have been interested in bees from at least the 1630s onwards as, alongside fellow horticultural author Gervase Markham, he authored one of the dedicatory poems to John Levett's *Ordering of Bees* (1634).[10]

BEES AND COMMON GOVERNANCE

The *Theatre* begins with an elegy to bees, celebrating them as 'the most excellent of all Insects whatsoever', noting their useful products, the intricacy of their physical forms, and their 'wisdome and invention', among other virtues.[11] Though Purchas cited authors from Pliny to Tertullian in support of these assertions, he did not hesitate to apply humanistic critiques, noting, for example, the dependence of Pliny, Varro and Columella on Aristotle, as well as denying some of their particular statements about bees, such as the assertion that bees carry stones as ballast on windy days.[12]

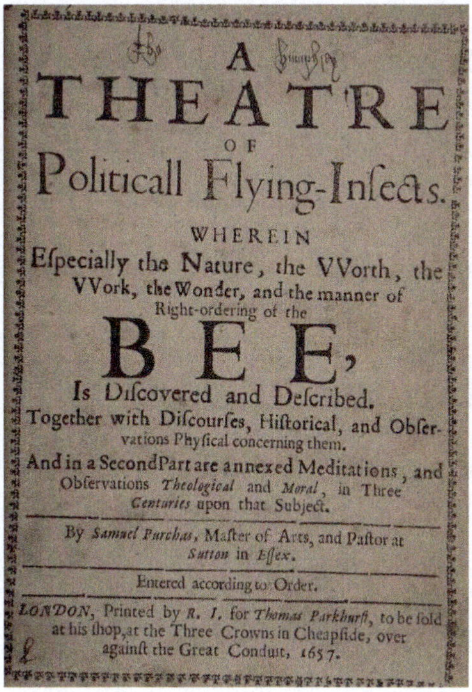

A
THEATRE
OF
Politicall Flying-Inſects.
WHEREIN
Eſpecially the Nature, the VVorth, the VVork, the Wonder, and the manner of Right-ordering of the
BEE,
Is Diſcovered and Deſcribed.
Together with Diſcourſes, Hiſtorical, and Obſervations Phyſical concerning them.
And in a SecondPart are annexed Meditations, and Obſervations *Theological* and *Moral*, in Three *Centuries* upon that Subject.
By *Samuel Purchas*, Maſter of Arts, and Paſtor at *Sutton* in *Eſſex*.
Entered according to Order.
LONDON, Printed by *R. I.* for *Thomas Parkhurſt*, to be ſold at his ſhop, at the Three Crowns in Cheapſide, over againſt the Great Conduit, 1657.

Figure 1: Frontispiece of Purchas's *Theatre of Politicall Flying-Insects.* Image: Wellcome Collection (https://creativecommons.org/publicdomain/mark/1.0)

Purchas also used the language of observation to challenge previous authors' statements about bees. For example, he refuted Aristotle's affirmation that bees were called to work by a set of 'buzzings', saying that 'no such exciting sound could I ever hear'.[13] Weiss has suggested that, given these observations, Purchas was likely a beekeeper himself.[14] It is a distinct possibility, given the first-hand language used throughout. In his description of bee anatomy, for instance, Purchas described them as having lungs, 'if my eyes deceive me not'.[15] In his description of the comb, he claimed expertise from his own observations to contradict the authority of an earlier author, Thomas Moffat, writing that 'had hee seriously viewed them [drones]', Moffat would have realized (as Purchas claimed) that drones could not, in fact, build combs.[16] Purchas also described first-hand experiences in his own 'Bee-garden', claiming to have hived more than forty swarms in his time.[17]

After addressing bees' types, senses and habits, the book moves on to discuss the governance of bees. Here, Purchas described bee society in somewhat unusual terms. One of the defining characteristics of bees in classical and Medieval literature was their loyalty; Pliny and Aristotle, for instance, argued that the 'king' bee never needed to use its sting because of the unquestioning devotion of its subjects. Purchas mentioned the bees' obedience only once, and in the context of an aphorism.[18] Rather, he emphasized their collectivity as their defining characteristic:

> They have one common respect, and reverence to their Commander by whose counsel their Commonwealth is governed; a common house, a common care of posterity, common labour, common food, common generation, a common use and fruition of all things.[19]

In this section, Purchas noted that the bees were united under a commander, but his constant repetition of 'common' moved the focus from their loyalty to the ruler to their loyalty to the commonwealth. He also used the terms 'king' or 'queen' less than many of his predecessors, a choice that Adam Ebert has suggested may have been due to the pressures of publishing during the Protectorate.[20] However, Purchas's view of the leader's role was as fundamentally precarious. In his discussion of this Commander, who he subsequently identified as a queen, he noted that:

> although they [the bees] are willingly subject to a leader, yet do they not altogether lose their liberty... if the Commons see it not convenient to diminish their numbers, upon the Queens grant, they kill the Probationer, and all of the Blood-royal; so that Prerogative avails little in the Commonwealth of Bees.[21]

Similarly, Purchas suggested that bees could merge hives 'with a general consent (except their generals, to whom such a resolution is deadly)'.[22] Given that England's own Commons had ordered the execution of the leader of the Blood-royal just eight years earlier, such a statement could hardly be read separately from the contemporary political situation. In fact given that, directly following this description, Purchas stated that 'the Polity of Bees is admirable and imitable', he could be seen as endorsing the current political state of affairs through an analogy between humans and bees.[23]

UNDERSTANDING BEES, UNDERSTANDING PEOPLE

For Purchas, the allegorical relationship between humans and bees provided not only a guide to human behaviour, but also a potential way of understanding the motives of bee-kind. In his discussion of queens, for example, he argued that the 'Commander' must not be 'an elected Governour; for the vulgar often want judgement in raising the worst and wickedest to the Throne'. At the same time, he denied that the queen was 'by hereditary succession placed in the Throne; for often through pleasures and flatteries are they rude and ignorant of true vertue'.[24] Rather, he suggested that the chief bee was the one who 'by nature hath hee the Sovereignty over all, excelling all in goodliness, and goodness, in mildness, and majesty'.[25] In this section, Purchas used an analogy with human experiences to better understand bees. Given the similarity between people and bees, he reasoned that if particular governance practices generated problems for one, they would do the same for the other.

In Purchas's view, investigating this allegory also provided a potential guide for human society. He wrote that 'the world is Gods Library, God manifested and drawn out; and all the creatures are as Glasses, in which we may see'.[26] In relation to bees specifically, he wrote that they had 'more than (almost) any' of 'Gods Majesty'.[27] Such an affirmation had precedents in classical and Christian literature; Aristotle argued that the 'genus of bees' had something divine about it, while Christian writers like the thirteenth-century Dominican friar Thomas of Cantimpré had framed bees as an example of the ideal communitarian life.[28] However, it appears that Purchas's view of the divine message being sent through bees was relatively literal, particularly when compared with the more general perspective on natural signs put forward by his Christian predecessors.[29] Purchas argued, for instance, that humans could model their leader-selection process on that of bees: 'what is Natures lesson, that the irrational creatures best express... for a civil man by natures rule is alwayes chiefe of the City, as the Commander among the Bees'.[30] While earlier Christian writers had allowed for natural signs that might bear little resemblance to the message they communicated, Purchas appears to be describing a world in which the same model, imprinted on Nature by divine force, should be used for both the government of people and of bees.

Such a reading may be indicative of a new type of natural theology emerging in the period. Around the beginning of the century, Francis Bacon had written that knowledge of God could be acquired 'by the contemplation of his Creatures'.[31] Purchas, who cited Bacon directly, would likely have been familiar with this theory.[32] His interpretation of it appears to have taken the form of searching for a model of governance shared by both humans and bees, a pattern accessible to human knowledge via observation. In some cases, this observation could be aided by technology and a Baconian emphasis on disrupting the normal course of nature, as when Purchas described the use of magnifiers in bee dissection.[33]

As such, Purchas' writing about bees represents a curious intersection of natural-philosophical methods and normative goals. By investigating bees through close observation, Purchas sought to generate insights that could be used to guide human society. Such a reading may support, as Katherine Calloway argues, the rise of a new type of observation-based natural philosophy in the seventeenth century.[34] Such an approach may also be linked to a Protestant-style approach to what Augustine had termed the 'Book of Nature'. As Scott Mandelbrote argues, a more literal view of the Bible's truths could be transposed to reading the Book of Nature; without the Catholic lens of allegory and symbolism, a Protestant might see a more straightforward correspondence between natural signs and their meanings.[35] In the case of bees, this could mean transposing their social organization onto humans, as Purchas appears in some instances to do. Purchas's work, aptly identified as a 'Physico-theological History of Bees' by one of its dedicatory poems, laid out a new model through which the study of nature could help humans align themselves better with the divine plan.[36]

MOSES RUSDEN'S *A FURTHER DISCOVERY OF BEES*

In 1657 Moses Rusden completed another major work on bees. Entitled *A Further Discovery of Bees*, this was as comprehensive as Samuel Purchas's: after beginning with a physical description of bees, Rusden then moved to discussing their society, virtues, generation, and husbandry. Like his predecessor, Rusden would hold bees up as a mirror to society. However, what he saw reflected there was very different.

In 1679, when the book was published, Rusden was 'Bee-Master' to King Charles II.[37] He was also linked with the Royal Society, whose experimental hives at Gresham College, Oxford, included the type of glass-sided hive that Rusden would describe in *Further Discovery.*[38] Rusden's variation on the glass-sided hive was octagonal, featuring glass panels covered by shutters that could be opened or closed according to the season and weather (Figure 2). This design, he assured his readers, was not only profitable, but also allowed observers to look in on the 'admirable workmanship of the Bees, which is very delightful to behold'.[39]

Unlike Purchas, Rusden did not begin his work with a paean to bees in general. Rather, he began by praising one bee in particular: 'the Royal Race of King-Bees, being natural Kings; one of them equals the value and worth of all the rest: therefore as the most worthy, I shall here describe the King Bee, as the first sort of Bees.'[40] The language of absolute monarchy pervades the work. The section 'On Government', for example, describes their social organization as follows:

> Their Government is in the person of the King... His Government is just; because he oppresseth none; the consequence of which is, unity throughout the whole Kingdom. His Government is absolute, because his orders are never disputed but obeyed. [41]

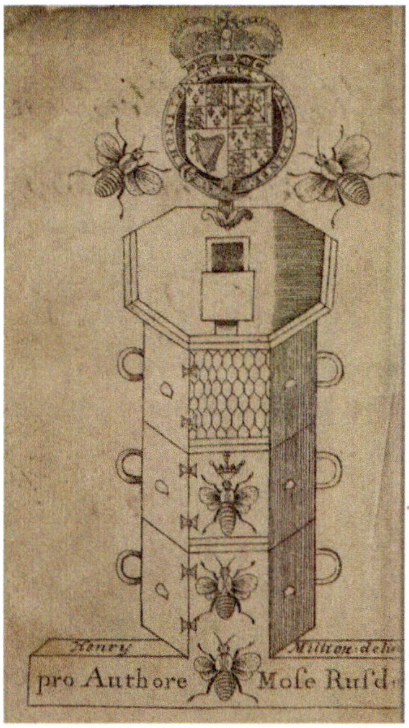

Figure 2. Rusden's glass-windowed box hive, as depicted in the *Further Discovery of Bees*. Image: Wellcome Collection (https://creativecommons.org/publicdomain/mark/1.0)

No trace of Purchas's rule of the commons is present in this description. For Rusden, the leader bee was the King in an absolutist sense: always obeyed, holder of all decision-making power. Rusden's kings were also hereditary. In his description of bee swarming – the same phenomenon described by Purchas as resulting in the 'diminishing of their numbers' – Rusden describes the bee that leads out the new swarm as a 'Prince', who is to assume leadership upon 'the loss or death of his Sire'.[42]

Rusden took this opportunity to stress both the harmony that ruled within the royal house of bees and their absolute power. For Rusden, the swarming process was a peaceful one, governed by the self-interest of the old ruler. For instance, he described the piping of the 'kings' before the swarming as a process of the old king giving 'his consent or orders' for the new king to depart with a swarm; if multiple new kings hatched at once, Rusden held that the older would either 'go himself, or send his younger Brother'.[43] Such a well-ordered, obedient view of swarming stands in strong contrast to classical accounts like that of Columella, who described the rise of multiple leaders as creating such opportunities for 'rebellion' and 'civil war' that any beekeeper who spotted multiple kings would be best advised to kill them immediately.[44]

Rusden explicitly challenged other readings of the swarm that would allow for communal power. He wrote, for instance, that Charles Butler's *Feminine Monarchie* was mistaken in supposing 'that the first Swarm went forth at the will of the Commons'.[45] He grounded this assertion not only in his own observations, but also in extrapolations of the logic of governance he attributed to the bees. According to Rusden, Butler thought that the first swarm must have been self-organizing because he did not hear any of the piping noises the leader bee usually made before a swarm's departure. Rusden argued that the lack of piping was actually because the old King would typically lead this first swarm, and he would have no need to issue orders to another leader 'when he intends to go himself.' The impossibility of self-organization was also implied by Rusden's affirmation that 'the King orders at once what the Bees readily execute in obedience thereunto'.[46] For Rusden, the bees must be following orders, because their perfect obedience made them incapable of doing anything else. The observed lack of piping, then, must be explainable as something other than an absence of orders; in this case, it was explainable as the provision of personal guidance.

OBSERVING THE VIRTUES OF BEES

In his description of swarming, as elsewhere in the work, Rusden placed a high value on first-hand experience. In his case this involved the active management of hives, particularly the ones in the royal gardens at St. James's Park. For example, the section entitled 'Of the Bees Loyalty to their King' recounts the experience of removing the king from one of the St. James's hives and the chaos that resulted:

> I took also the King-Bee which was in the uppermost Hive at that time.... the first work they [the bees] did (as is their custom) was upon this disturbance to see if their King were safe, and among them; (whom I still kept from them) and missing their King, presently some fly abroad to seek him, some crept, and others ran up and down, as men in a tumult, or like unto persons distracted... I have also done the like, and had the same effect with several Colonies.[47]

Such affirmations are repeated throughout the text; for example, in response to the Aristotelian affirmation that the ruling bees never use their stings, Rusden wrote that 'I have had about twenty King-Bees in my hands this last year, and could provoke but two of them to put forth their stings, unless they were hurt'.[48] This sort of first-hand investigation seems to have had two main aspects for Rusden. One may be seen as 'experimental' in a Baconian sense; by disrupting the normal course of nature, Rusden was able to observe things about bees, such as the disinclination of king bees to sting, that could not otherwise have been seen.

This model was also linked to the use of technology, as the experiment described above was made possible by Rusden's use of a windowed box hive, a beekeeping technology that seems to have been invented around the mid-century.[49] Rusden based his design on the recently-patented glass hive of John Gedde who, in turn, drew the idea of 'transparent Hives' from Dr Wilkins, identified as the 'late Bishop of Chester'.[50] Wilkins's hive, in its turn, was based on that of William Mewe, an Oxford divine whose writings on bees and glass hives appeared in Samuel Hartlib's mid-century *Reformed Common-Wealth of Bees.*[51]

The other aspect of Rusden's personal experience with bees was a demonstrative one. The experiment that involved removing the king bee, mentioned above, was performed for 'the admiration of all that were present', an audience that reportedly comprised 'The Kings Majesty and some Persons of Honour'.[52] This action indicates the use of bees as an illustrative method, in this case of the idea of true monarchy. Such an approach may be seen as similar to that of the sixteenth-century Jesuit, Athanasius Kircher, who used his collection of curiosities – one of Europe's largest – to illustrate divine messages imprinted in natural things.[53] It may also be seen in some of Rusden's predecessors: William Mewe, for example, described his hives as a 'Hyerogliphick of Labour', suggesting that the bees could serve as an emblem or natural sign, divinely designed to demonstrate a particular principle to humankind.[54]

The accent on observation as an activity points to a subtly different view of the theological implications of studying bees than that put forward by Purchas. James Joseph Bono, writing on Rusden's contemporary and fellow glass-hive owner Robert Boyle, has suggested that one version of a 'literal', Protestant-inflected approach to the Book of Nature could be an increased emphasis on first-hand observation as a religious activity.[55] Just as a Biblical critic would need to get as close to the original texts as possible, the reader of the Book of Nature would need to observe natural phenomena with minimal mediation. Rusden's interest in glass hives may be seen as pointing to just such a perspective on the importance of observation. Glass-panelled hives, which allowed people to witness the day-to-day activities of bees at close quarters, would be adopted by thinkers like John Evelyn, in whose spiritually oriented garden they would serve a contemplative purpose (Figure 3).[56] Such an approach, which privileged the act of observation, was not incompatible with one that saw bees as a model for human society; Evelyn, also a committed monarchist, would call his bees 'a Lecture of obedience to Rebells'.[57] Rusden bridged these two visions of the religious implications of studying bees, creating a hive that would turn the garden into demonstration space even while leaving open the possibility that they could generate specific insights applicable to the contemporary political situation.

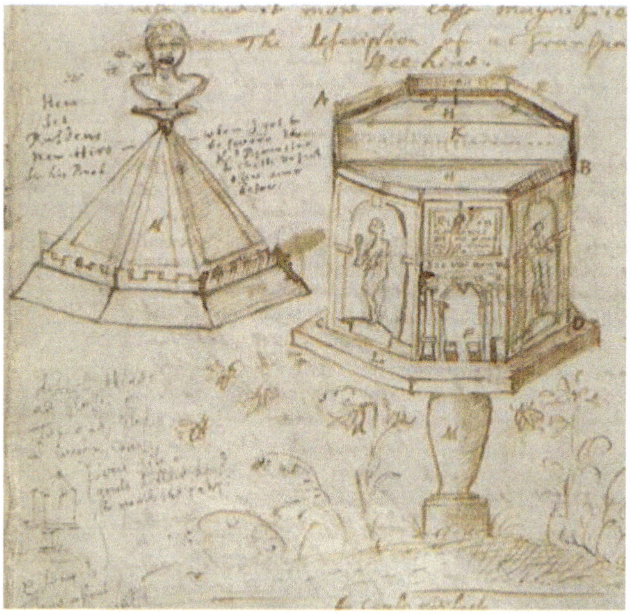

Figure 3. John Evelyn's glass beehive, based on William Mewe's design.
British Library ADD MS 78342, f.212v.

CONCLUSION

In the seventeenth century, English writers turned to bees as a potential way to understand how people should be governed. In so doing, they combined a centuries-old Christian tradition of understanding nature as an expression of the divine with new techniques of manipulating and investigating nature. The results of this were a new, quasi-experimental theology, one that elevated the value of observing the natural world first-hand as a way of accessing divine truths. These truths, demonstrated or discovered through observation, could then be applied to human society in order to improve it.

However, this new study of bees could produce markedly different results. Samuel Purchas's *Theatre of Politicall Flying-Insects*, composed and published during the final years of the Protectorate, painted a vision of society that, while far from democratic, ought to be ruled by the 'commons'. By observing aspects of bee behaviour that served communal aims, and by projecting aspects of human reasonings onto bees, Purchas produced a description of a society that was far from monarchical. In his highly detailed study, Purchas also identified aspects of bee behaviour, such as their selection of a civil leader, that he recommended for direct transposition onto human society. Such a perspective marked a distinct departure from Medieval Christian writings about bees, which had used nature to illustrate, rather than investigate, the divine plan.

In contrast, Moses Rusden, writing under the Restoration government of Charles II, saw a world in which bees stood for the divinely ordained monarchy. Focusing on examples in which bees were particularly dedicated to their leader, Rusden produced an illustration of a peaceful, stable, natural monarchy congruent with the prevailing political climate and the needs of his patron. By creating a glass-panelled beehive in which all these virtues were visible to the naked eye, Rusden also allowed the observation of bees to take on greater value as an activity in its own right.

For both authors, though, the language of first-hand observation was paramount. Both challenged statements about bees made by classical and Medieval writers, invoking their own experience as a source of authority. And for both, bee and human societies were analogous in more than just a literary sense. The wellspring of both was a natural, divinely ordained model of governance; this fundamental kinship allowed them to relate the behaviour of one to the other. It also allowed for the unification of natural philosophy with theology, using the study of nature to produce insights into the divine plan. Over the next century, this interest in natural particulars would come to form the basis of modern natural theology. For politically interested writers in the seventeenth century, theology provided a route to an observational 'political science', one in which careful study was capable not only of describing the world, but of shaping it for the better.

REFERENCES

[1] David J. Depew, 'Humans and Other Political Animals in Aristotle's "History of Animals"', *Phronesis*, 40:2 (1995), pp. 156–81.

[2] On European beekeeping, see Eva Crane, *The World History of Beekeeping and Honey Hunting*, Beekeeping and Honey Hunting (New York: Routledge, 1999).

[3] Jonathan Woolfson, 'The Renaissance of Bees', *Renaissance Studies,* 24:2 (2010), pp.281-300 (p.299); Elizabeth Crachiolo, 'Queen Bees, Queen Bess, and the Gender Politics of Butler's Feminine Monarchie', *The Sixteenth Century Journal*, 49:2 (2018), p. 323.

[4] Pedro Mexio, *The Treasurie of Auncient and Moderne Times· Containing the Learned Collections, Iudicious Readings, and Memorable Obseruations: Not Onely Diuine, Morrall and Phylosophicall. But Also Poeticall, Martiall, Politicall, Historicall, Astrologicall, &c. Translated out of That Worthy Spanish Gentleman, Pedro Mexio.* (London: Printed by W. Iaggard, 1613), p. 660.

[5] Baldassare Castiglione, *The Book of the Courtier, by Count Baldesar Castiglione*, trans. by Leonard Epstein Opdycke (London: Duckworth, 1902), pp. 260-61.

[6] Nicole A. Jacobs, *Bees in Early Modern Transatlantic Literature: Sovereign Colony* (Milton, UK: Taylor & Francis Group, 2021), Introduction and Chapter 4.

[7] On the early modern project of studying the divine in nature, see Margaret J. Osler, *Reconfiguring the World: Nature, God, and Human Understanding from the Middle Ages to Early Modern Europe* (Baltimore: Johns Hopkins University Press, 2010), pp. 39-40; James Joseph Bono, *The Word of God and the Languages of Man: Interpreting Nature in Early Modern Science and Medicine* (Madison: University of Wisconsin Press, 1995), pp. 70-75.

[8] Samuel Purchas, *A Theatre of Politicall Flying-Insects Wherein Especially the Nature, the worth, the work, the wonder, and the Manner of Right-Ordering of the Bee, Is Discovered and Described* (London: Printed by R. I. for Thomas Parkhurst, 1657), p. 2.

[9] Harry B. Weiss, 'Samuel Purchas and His "Theatre of Politicall Flying Insects"', *Journal of the New York Entomological Society*, 34:1 (1926), pp. 71–77 (p. 75).

[10] John Levett, *The Ordering of Bees: Or, The True History of Managing Them from Time to Time, with Their Hony and Waxe, Shewing Their Nature and Breed as Also What Trees, Plants, and Hearbs Are Good for Them, and Namely What Are Hurtfull* (London, Printed by Thomas Harper for John Harison, 1634).

[11] Purchas, pp. 1-2.

[12] Purchas, pp. 8-11.

[13] Purchas, pp. 8-11.

[14] Weiss, p. 73.

[15] Purchas, p. 37.

[16] Purchas, pp. 39, 60. Thomas Moffat's *Insectorum sive minimorum Animalium Theatrum* had been published, posthumously, in 1634, Moffat having died in 1604.

[17] Pliny, *Historia naturalis*, XI.17; Aristotle, *Historia animalium*, V.21.

[18] Purchas, p. 340.

[19] Purchas, p. 17.

[20] Adam Ebert, 'Nectar for the Taking: The Popularization of Scientific Bee Culture in England, 1609–1809', *Agricultural History*, 85:3 (2011), pp. 322–43 (p. 328).

[21] Purchas, p. 33.

[22] Purchas, p. 16.

[23] Purchas, p. 17.

[24] Purchas, p. 16.

[25] Purchas, p. 17.

[26] Purchas, Epistle Dedicatory, p. 2.

[27] Purchas, Epistle Dedicatory, p. 3.

[28] Daryn Lehoux, 'Why Does Aristotle Think Bees Are Divine? Proportion, Triplicity and Order in the Natural World', *The British Journal for the History of Science*, 52.3 (2019), 383–403; Julia Burkhart, 'Learning from Bees, Wasps, and Ants: Communal Norms, Social Practices, and Contingencies of Nature in Medieval Insect Allegories', in *Fragmented Nature: Medieval Latinate Reasoning on the Natural World and Its Order*, ed. by Mattia Cipriani and Nicola Polloni, Studies in Medieval History and Culture (New York: Routledge, 2022), pp. 93–110.

[29] For a contrary opinion, see Ebert, p. 339. On signs in general, see Gerrit Jasper Schenk, 'Disastro, Catastrophe, and Divine Judgment: Words, Concepts and Images for "Natural" Threats to Social Order in the Middle Ages and Renaissance', in *Disaster, Death and the Emotions in the Shadow of the Apocalypse, 1400–1700*, ed. by Jennifer Spinks and Charles Zika, Palgrave Studies in the History of Emotions (London: Palgrave Macmillan UK, 2016), pp. 45–67.

[30] Purchas, p. 17.

[31] See Scott Mandelbrote, 'Early Modern Natural Theologies', in *The Oxford Handbook of Natural Theology*, ed. by Russell Re Manning, John Hedley Brooke, and Fraser Watts (Oxford: Oxford University Press, 2013), pp. 75-99 (p. 88).

[32] See Purchas's reference to what the "L. Verulam supposeth' about the humming of bees as well as his natural philosophy more generally, pp. 100, 111 and pp. 128, 131 respectively.
[33] Purchas, p. 14.
[34] Katherine Calloway, *Natural Theology in the Scientific Revolution: God's Scientists*, Pickering Studies in Philosophy of Religion (London: Pickering & Chatto, 2014), Introduction.
[35] Mandelbrote, pp. 66-67.
[36] Poem by N.F. in Purchas, Elegies, p.1.
[37] Eva Crane, 'Recent Research on the World History of Beekeeping', *Bee World,* 80:4 (1999), pp. 174-86 (p. 179).
[38] Moses Rusden, *A Further Discovery of Bees Treating of the Nature, Government, Generation & Preservation of the Bee. With the Experiments and Improvements, Arising from the Keeping Them in Transparent Boxes, Instead of Straw-Hives* (London, printed for the author and H. Million, 1679), Epistle Dedicatory.
[39] Rusden, p.84.
[40] Rusden, pp. 1-2.
[41] Rusden, pp. 21-2.
[42] Rusden, p. 26.
[43] Rusden, p. 26.
[44] 'Sunt enim saepe plures unius populi duces, et quasi procerum seditione plebs in partes diducitur: quod frequenter fieri prohibendum est, quoniam intestino bello totae gentes consumuntur. Itaque si constat principibus gratia, manet pax incruenta. Sin autem saepius acie dimicantes notaveris, duces seditionum interficere curabis: dimicantium vero proelia praedictis remediis sedantur.' Columella, *De re rustica,* IX.9.
[45] Rusden, pp. 25-6.
[46] Rusden, p. 26.
[47] Rusden, p. 30.
[48] Rusden, p. 4.
[49] Crane, *The World History of Beekeeping and Honey Hunting,* pp. 405-7; see also designs in Samuel Hartlib, *The Reformed Common-Wealth of Bees* (London: Printed for Giles Calvert, 1655), pp. 8, 14, 52.
[50] Rusden, Epistle Dedicatory.
[51] Mewe described sending instructions for how to replicate his hive to Wilkins – see Hartlib, p. 41. For Mewe's design, see Hartlib, pp. 41-51; on the link between Mewe and Rusden via Gedde see D. J. Bryden, 'John Gedde's Bee-House and the Royal Society', *Notes and Records of the Royal Society of London*, 48:2 (1994): pp. 193–213 (p. 194).
[52] Rusden, pp. 29-30.
[53] On Kircher's Museum, see Koen Vermeir, 'Athanasius Kircher's Magical Instruments: An Essay on "Science", "Religion" and Applied Metaphysics', *Studies in History and Philosophy of Science Part A*, 38:2 (2007), pp. 363–400.
[54] For the reference to the hive as a 'Hyeroglyphic' see Hartlib, p. 42. On emblems and hieroglyphics as natural signs, see William Ashworth, "Natural History and the Emblematic World View," in David C. Lindberg and Robert S. Westman, *Reappraisals of the Scientific Revolution* (Cambridge: Cambridge University Press, 1990), pp. 303-32; John Manning, *The Emblem* (London: Reaktion, 2002).
[55] James J. Bono, 'Reading Literally: Boyle, the Bible, and the Book of Nature', in *The Palgrave Handbook of Early Modern Literature and Science*, ed. by Howard Marchitello and Evelyn Tribble, Palgrave Handbooks of Literature and Science (London: Palgrave Macmillan UK, 2017), pp. 179–207 (p. 187).
[56] For Evelyn on bees, see John Evelyn, *Elysium Britannicum, or The Royal Gardens*, ed. by John E. Ingram (Philadelphia: University of Pennsylvania Press, 2001), pp. 270-80.
[57] Evelyn, p. 274.

3

GREENING RESPONSES TO CRISIS AND CATASTROPHE

The term greening is used to indicate the process of making an environment greener and more environmentally friendly by introducing trees and other plants. The term is also used to indicate policies that are sustainable and environmentally friendly. Today, greening is accepted as a scientifically proven means of countering the effects of global warming.[1]

Two radically different paths to urban greening are explored in this chapter. One paper discusses the Garden City policies of Singapore's government; the other describes the growth of urban agriculture in Detroit in the absence of any policy dealing with urban decline.

In the late 1960s, when the government of newly independent Singapore set out to create a new and modern nation it adopted the idea of the 'garden city'. Tree planting and greening were integral to urban development, to a strategy for attracting foreign investment and to the aim of fostering a sense of a national identity.

Since the late 1990s the Garden City project has evolved but never at the cost of losing the focus on greening. Detroit's story has been entirely different. In the early 2000s the buildings and infrastructure of post-industrial Detroit were crumbling and weeds taking hold in large swathes of derelict land. While the city authorities were occupied with a financial crisis that eventually led to bankruptcy, individuals, community and other groups started to clear the weeds and grow food on vacant land. These grass roots initiatives grew into a vibrant urban farming movement in what could be termed a policy vacuum. Since 2018, however, the authorities have introduced and now support a variety of greening initiatives.

[1] Chi Chen, Dan Li, *et al,* 'Biophysical impacts of Earth greening largely controlled by aerodynamic resistance', *Sciences Advances,* 6:47 (November 2020). Available from https://www.science.org/doi/10.1126/sciadv.abb1981

SINGAPORE'S GARDEN CITY: THE POLITICAL LANGUAGE OF URBAN PLANTING

JESSE O'NEILL

ABSTRACT

The idea of Singapore as a 'garden city' was created in the late 1960s, shortly after Singapore gained independent statehood. Bearing little direct relationship to the earlier Garden City Movement, it aimed to transform Singapore's urban landscape into a clean and green international city. This paper considers the idea of the garden city as a political tool, which acted as a government-led approach to urban management that pursued aims of modernization and nation building. The policy's origins in the tree planting campaign of the early 1960s, and how the shortcomings of that scheme informed the state's later approaches to the garden city, are discussed. The relationships between the garden city and other social reform campaigns of the 1970s are considered and the expansion of the garden city policy into newer strategies of urban planning is explored. More than just creating a landscape of urban greenery, the garden policy became the model for Singapore's wider economic and social reforms, shaping the long-term success of what began as an uncertain postcolonial nation.

INTRODUCTION

Singapore is a dense city-state with modern architecture and abundant tropical vegetation that has long been labelled a 'garden city'. The term has been used since the late 1960s to promote Singapore to international investors and tourists, as well as to shape how Singaporeans themselves understand their built environment and national identity. I have previously argued that the idea of a garden city in Singapore, which began in 1967 with aims of cleaning and greening the urban landscape, quickly became a shorthand for any experience of a convenient and relaxed modern lifestyle that resulted from the physical and social transformations introduced by Singapore's government after becoming an independent nation in 1965.[1] Other authors have addressed the subject through similar lines of thought, variously positioning the garden city as representing economic growth, being an index of changing urban planning processes, illustrating government foresight, or demonstrating the Singaporean government's authoritarian sense of control.[2]

Evidently, Singapore's garden city is about much more than urban planning and laying out gardens. It reflects a decades-long political policy of creating an image of urban life that supported state ambitions of modernizing infrastructure and economic development. In Singapore, the garden city was investment in a political language of national security and growth, but this is not the only approach to understanding the state's environmental, physical and economic planning. In this chapter I sketch a wider history of the garden city in Singapore, looking to earlier policy that informed it, and later policies that extended it.

PLANTING AN IDEA

Singapore's ambition to be a garden city was established on 11 May 1967, when prime minister Lee Kuan Yew introduced the idea to government workers in the Cleansing Department.[3] Once they had cleaned the city and instilled ideas of urban hygiene, they would proceed to make the place beautiful with trees and shrubbery. This was not the first use of the 'garden city' in Singapore; it had been applied earlier in localized garden suburb developments like the Wah Garden City of 1923, which drew directly from the English Garden City Movement.[4] However, Lee's speech showed no direct connection to that earlier movement or its key figures. Instead, this was a proposal for a new context of decolonization, responding to the desire to establish a new and successful nation.

Lee's 1967 speech was not his first attempt to establish a state-sponsored planting programme. While coordinated planting schemes existed in Singapore's Rural Board as early as the mid-1950s, Lee, who had been prime minister since home rule was achieved in 1959, launched his own campaign for urban planting in 1963. This programme promised that the government would plant 5,000 trees, and it implored city residents to plant an equal number themselves.[5] The campaign began with Lee planting an Angsana (*Pterocarpus indicus*) in his constituency, an event which marked the beginning of the Singaporean government's longstanding involvement in horticultural bureaucracy.[6]

At this time, Lee and his People's Action Party were attempting to reform Singapore in anticipation of its decolonization and joining with the Malaysian union. The recently established Housing and Development Board was moving people out of urban squalor and into modern housing developments, and the Jurong Town Corporation was beginning to industrialize the city's economy and workforce. The early 1960s saw dramatic transformations in the built environment which meant extensive land clearance and new construction. At the launch of the tree planting campaign, it was estimated that for every ten trees cut down, only one was being planted.

Interestingly, though, the reason given for the first tree planting campaign had nothing to do with beautifying the urbanizing city, countering the effects of industrial growth, or softening modern architectural styles. In the following decades, these were common reasons given for the value of the garden city, but in 1963 ministers were determined to explain that there was nothing that could be deemed superficial about their interests in tree planting.[7] Instead, they claimed that the importance of trees lay with the need for water. They proposed that more trees encouraged cloud formation and moisture retention, thereby increasing rainfall and improving the island's water supply.[8] Despite the opening of Singapore's municipal reservoir in 1878, the island had never been able to store and provide enough water, relying on piped water from the neighbouring Malayan state of Johor, and in the 1960s water security was still a key concern.[9] For Singapore's government, greenery was never an end in itself, it always had other motivations.

ESTABLISHING THE GARDEN CITY

From its start, politicians and community leaders became the faces of the tree planting campaign, regularly being photographed going out and planting saplings themselves.[10] But it was always intended that the public should take an equal role in the initiative. This did not really happen. Early in 1967, the Ministry of National Development declared the tree planting campaign unsuccessful, partly because it lacked expert botanical advice, and partly because the public had shown that they did not yet care for trees.[11] The campaign needed to be relaunched. In April a new National Tree and Parks Committee was formed, an aim of which was to advise on encouraging popular interest in gardening. And in May the prime minister launched the Garden City policy, which absorbed tree planting within a larger framework for establishing order, cleanliness, and greenery within the city.

After the Garden City's launch, various branches of Singapore's government were quick to act. By September the Housing and Development Board was already giving more attention to tree planting on its estates, though they still noted a need to cover saplings with barbed wire to protect them from inconsiderate residents.[12] A specialized Trees and Plants Unit was then established within the Public Works Department,[13] and by October they had already planted 9,000 new trees.[14] To provide all the plants that would be needed for roadside planting, the Botanic Gardens transformed parts of their grounds into nurseries that supported government building and landscaping.[15] From the start of the policy, responsibility for realizing the Garden City fell to many government departments – parks offices, housing bodies, the Public Works Department, and the Ministries of Health and National Development. At first, there was no centralized plan other than a drive for rapid planting. This drew criticism in a parliamentary debate at the end of 1967, when backbenchers claimed the policy was un-coordinated and often ineffective.[16] But the government's aim in this initial phase was for visible results as soon as possible, showing the public that there was a real prospect of urban transformation. This view also defined the plants that were used. The Chief Parks Officer, Tan Peng Gee, explained that the trees preferred for public planting were not necessarily the most beautiful, but were practical. For urban roadsides Pride of India (*Koelreuteria paniculata*), Yellow Flame (*Peltophorum pterocarpum*), and Pong Pong (*Cerbera odollam*) were preferred, all of them fast-growing and 'upright and compact'.[17]

As official planting continued, greater concern was given to popular engagement, the absence of which had resulted in failure for the 1963 planting scheme. The Garden City was launched with a call for Singaporeans to take on increased personal responsibility for maintaining a clean, healthy and green

Figure 1. Cover of *Selected Plants and Planting for a Garden City: Forty Shrubs* (1971), published by the Singapore Ministry of National Development. Author's collection.

environment. Though rather than just by requesting public help, this time engagement was achieved through a gradual series of legal measures and highly visible community events. Fines for littering and damaging public plants were greatly increased, a neighbourhood-watch programme for garden vandalism was set up, and in the early 1970s tax cuts were introduced for people planting and maintaining gardens of their own.[18] Community centres organized cleaning days in local areas, and competitions between housing estates aimed to reward those who could create the cleanest and most beautiful housing blocks, drawing the image of modern architecture into the sphere of the Garden City.[19] Teachers were given the duty of teaching children to respect plants, and their students were given plants to care for at home, which allowed them to also instruct their families in the values of gardening.[20] Further plant nurseries were established along Dunearn Road to provide for the public, turning this street into 'the floral mile'.[21] And at the start of the 1970s the Ministry of National Development entered the business of publishing gardening books, teaching the public about the forty species preferred for Singapore's Garden City (Figure 1).

In 1971, as public engagement with the garden city seemed increasingly secure, the government decided to relaunch its tree planting campaign by creating an annual Tree Planting Day (Figure 2). These days became major events throughout the 1970s, where individuals and community groups would plant tens of thousands of trees across the city in a single day.[22] In the weeks leading up to Tree Planting Day, nurseries on the floral mile cut prices of saplings by as much as half, hoping to boost engagement with mass planting.

Figure 2. Minister for Culture, Jek Yeun Thong, planting a tree on Tree Planting Day at East Coast Park (1974). Ministry of Information and the Arts Collection: courtesy of National Archives of Singapore.

THE POLITICS OF GARDENING

Between launching the tree planting campaign in 1963 and the Garden City in 1967, Singapore's political situation had changed dramatically. In 1963, Singapore prepared to cast off its British colonial status and join the new nation of Malaysia. By 1967, Singapore had joined Malaysia, been caught in the confrontation between Malaysia and Indonesia, seen race riots, left the Malaysian union, and become its own independent city-state. Combined with pre-existing housing and economic crises, heightened concern for its water supply, and a vague concern about a Malaysian invasion, Singaporean politics in the late 1960s pursued a 'survivalist' mode that aspired to securing national unity. It was a period when the government attempted to reinvent Singapore to ensure its security, and the Garden City was a key tool for achieving this.

If the public fully engaged in the Garden City policy by planting and maintaining gardens themselves, it was hoped that they would then develop a greater sense of commitment to the progress of the new nation. As Goh Hong Yi proposes, the idea of a 'green' Singapore became a strategy for nation building.[23] Since gardening takes work and demands regular care, they would become rooted in the fortunes of Singapore, and less likely to associate with ancestral homelands or view themselves as citizens of other countries. Although it was suggested in research from the early 1970s that the government often overestimated any attachments to these distant homelands, the state still aimed to invent a new idea for what it meant to be Singaporean.[24] Survivalist politics essentially created an ambition for social engineering.

A united Singaporean people, however, was not enough. Prior to the merger with Malaysia, it had been determined that Singapore's economy was not strong enough to survive on its own. Now that Singapore was alone, economic growth was urgent. As the state sought to draw international investment and expand its manufacturing sector, the presentation of Singapore as an ordered and clean city, whose citizens contributed to national improvement and showed respect for their environment, was seen as contributing to the state's financial security. As early as 1965 Lee Kwan Yew had spoken of his 'visions of a beautiful garden' that 'would be bearing gold and silver underneath'.[25] Planting gardens was therefore viewed as a means of creating order that would draw wealth and provide security. As a part of this way of thinking, the modernized garden city was also seen as a draw for tourists. In the 1970s, tourism promotions were launched in Japan, which portrayed 'Singapore as a garden city that is beautiful, a safe place for female tourists, and a heaven for shoppers.'[26]

In this way, the idea of the garden city was becoming an elastic term. From its beginnings it literally referred to increased planting and a green city environment. Over time, it also came to infer ideas of cleanliness, modernization, economic development, a respectful population, and order. Broadly, it represented the scope of the famous motif put forward by Lee Kuan Yew, that Singapore had transformed from a 'third-world' to a 'first-world' nation. However, the Garden City policy did not lay out all the requirements for this complete social and economic transformation, and to achieve this the government began launching a rolling series of campaigns that each aimed to alter people and city in smaller ways.

At the end of the 1970s, writers at *Berita Harian*, Singapore's Malay-language newspaper, began complaining about the number of official campaigns and the confusion that they thought could result.[27] They referred to Singapore as a 'campaign nation', questioning the effectiveness of running so many at the same time. The writers went so far as to suggest these showed the heavy-handedness of a government that did not trust its population to know what is important. There was no doubt that there had been benefits from these campaigns, but they questioned whether there had really been lasting effects, since old habits often resumed once the campaign had ended. By this time there had been campaigns for tree-planting, road safety, saving electricity, saving water, health, the metric system, and speaking Mandarin. There had been the Use Your Hands campaign, the Keep Singapore Clean campaign, the Sports for All campaign, Gracious Living, and its follow-up, the Courtesy campaign. Each addressed a particular matter of social, economic, or political necessity, intending to reform some small part of modern life in Singapore.

I would argue that in comparison to the other campaigns, the Garden City was somewhat different. It began with direct and practical ambitions, promoting the cleaning and greening of the city; however, in implementation these elements were separately covered by the tree planting campaign and the Ministry of Health's 'Keep Singapore Clean' campaign. The Garden City was therefore wider than these individual campaigns, addressing modernization and national identity, and over time it connected with a range of these smaller campaigns. Whereas individual campaigns targeted specific behaviours, the Garden City provided an overarching vision for what Singapore could become – connecting the various campaigns and giving them roles within a wider national aspiration. For example, the aim to re-invent Singaporeans as a hard-working and 'rugged' people was intended to create a workforce that would help draw international manufacturing industries to Singapore.[28] This informed the promotion of mass participation in sport and exercise as a national duty, which became the Sports for All campaign in 1973. This campaign established a need for sporting grounds and accessible open spaces that would be provided by the urban planning principles deriving from the Garden City. If the initial phase of the Garden City was criticized as un-coordinated, after several years it had become a highly unified system of interrelated policies, programmes, and social reforms.

As a broader policy for urban and social development, the Garden City wove together and contained smaller campaigns, acting as a guiding principle not only for planting but for state development. Where many other campaigns had positive results but not measurable output, the Garden City had a quantifiable measure of success through the planting of trees and the percentage of land occupied by green spaces. As Timothy P. Barnard and Corinne Heng have said, 'nature had become a metaphor for Singaporean development. It was to be tamed and directed, much like the populace'.[29] In many ways, the visibility of trees, shrubs and flowers, whether planted by state departments or residents, demonstrated the extent to which the population supported the government's plans and methods, and thus the extent to which they adhered to the wider range of campaigns. The Garden City was really an all-encompassing approach to national development and social reform, where trees could become a measure of success. And as the idea of the garden became firmly entrenched, it increasingly featured as an aspect of national identity, which was reinforced through architecture, tourism campaigns, government graphics such as the Wayside Trees stamp series (Figure 3), Chingay parades at Chinese New Year (Figure 4), and National Day parades.

Figure 3. Wayside Trees of Singapore, stamp series showing the Yellow Flame, Cabbage Tree, Rose of India, and Variegated Coral Tree.[30] Designed by Tay Siew Chiah (1976). Author's collection.

Figure 4. The 'Our Garden City' float in the Chingay Procession (1991). Ministry of Information and the Arts Collection: courtesy of National Archives of Singapore.

GROWING THE GARDEN CITY

In the early 1980s, newspapers announced that the government was initiating a second phase to the Garden City. There would be more flowering plants, more colour, more fruit-bearing trees, and generally a more beautiful appearance in the city. But, as Barnard and Heng suggest, we might actually consider this second phase as having begun earlier, in 1975, since that year seems to mark a transition from the amateur aims of rapid planting to a more refined and expert-driven approach to gardening.[31]

The lack of expert botanists early in the garden city efforts had been noted, but at that time it hardly mattered, because the greater concern was to gain public support, but by the mid-1970s the rhetoric of the garden city was firmly established. At the beginning of the decade the Botanic Gardens, recognizing the need for specialists, established a new diploma for Ornamental Horticulture and Landscape Design that was based on the Diploma in Horticulture launched at Kew Gardens in 1963.[32] In 1973, the Parks and Trees Unit of the Public Works Department combined with the scientific experts at the Botanic Gardens under the oversight of the Ministry of National Development, being reorganized in 1975 as the Parks and Recreation Department. It was the gradual development of expertise from the middle of the 1970s that allowed the introduction of the public 'second phase' in the 1980s. This resulted in the common sight of flower bushes on road overpasses (Figure 5), the introduction of vertical planting on new buildings like the Shangri-La Hotel (considered the epitome of the Garden City at the start of the 1980s)[33] and the development of major new parks.

Figure 5. Pedestrian overpass planted with colourful flowers as part of 'phase two' of Singapore's garden city policy (c.1985–1990). Ministry of Information and the Arts Collection: courtesy of National Archives of Singapore.

It was also in the 1980s, however, that ideas about the natural environment began changing. While it was beyond question that the Garden City policy had transformed Singapore's physical environment, often for the better, environmental groups such as the Nature Society began taking aim at the precarious notion of 'nature' that developed under this model. They made the point that the 'garden' had become artificial, reflecting little of the original natural conditions of Southeast Asia. They argued that in many ways the attempt to create a 'garden city' acted as an attempt to fight against ecology and replace it with an invented and controlled landscape that was more about accommodating modern buildings than it was about plants, animals, and natural systems.[34] These movements would later have an effect on Singapore's landscape policies, but they took time to be accepted. In the meantime, urban development continued under the older model, where manicured garden landscapes expanded around the new towns that spread across the span of the island.

An expansion of the Garden City method was proposed in 1991 by Liu Thai Ker, head of the Urban Redevelopment Authority, which he called the 'Green and Blue Plan'.[35] This proposed an interconnected network of park and water spaces to frame urban townships. It also defined the types of green spaces that would be considered, including natural areas, major public parks, adventure parks and sports fields. Importantly, and central to the proposal, the model established the idea of 'boundary separators', which were to be green linking spaces that connected major parks and served as green belts to define the limits of urban areas. The image created by the proposal was one of distinct city estates and neighbourhoods that existed as urban islands within a larger network of parkland. Here, parks no longer existed just as elements within urban areas, but rather, the urban areas existed within a larger contiguous parkland – reversing the hierarchy of the earlier garden city. The idea was transformative; the news article that reported the proposal commented that Singapore would, as a result, soon look more like a 'city in a garden' than a garden city. That title – the 'city in a garden' – was adopted by Singapore's government as an official replacement of the Garden City policy in 1998.[36]

Criticisms of the new model echoed those of the Garden City – namely that it was the planned obliteration of nature in favour of the controlled simulacrum of the garden.[37] But the policy endured, resulting in more artificial construction of nature within and around urban areas. At the turn of the century, a large part of the 'city in a garden policy' resulted in new approaches to architectural development that made use of vegetative façades on buildings. This has defined the urban environment in Singapore for the past two decades, with green walls, rooftop gardens, and sky terraces turning architecture itself into a new site for garden growth. In 2002 the Minister for National Development,

Figure 6. View of Supertree Grove, designed by Grant Associates, which sits in the larger Gardens by the Bay, designed by Wilkinson Eyre (2012): courtesy of National Archives of Singapore.

Mah Bow Tan addressed this idea as a tension between land scarcity and the desire for greenery, aiming for 'more greenery skywards [...] to ameliorate the harsh and stark concrete facade' of contemporary buildings.[38] This led to architectural firms creating buildings that expanded the natural vegetative capacity of the sites they worked with, greater connections between existing parks, and new icons of the architectural landscape that promoted the urban garden, such as Gardens by the Bay in 2012, and the Jewel in 2019 (Figure 6).

RETURNING TO NATURE

Although they may have had little effect on urban policy early on, the arguments of environmentalist movements did in time begin to shape understandings of the city and its connections with nature. In 2005, parliament passed a law strengthening the powers of the National Parks Board, giving them oversight for new developments in relation to plant loss, raising fines for developers' illegal cutting, and aiming to strengthen conservation laws.[39] And, there was a notable increase in the green cover of Singapore island, from 37.5 per cent in 1986 to 46.5 per cent in 2007, although it was noted that most of this was artificial, with primary and secondary forest only occupying 2.5 per cent of land.[40]

However, recognition of the distinction between the natural environment and the artificial garden has recently produced another policy shift. In mid-2020, the 'city in a garden' policy gave way to the new policy of the 'city in nature'. Like previous shifts, this will come with an expanded programme of new nature pathways, gardens and tree plantings, and is also being framed as a response to climate change and the need to clarify divisions between nature reserves and areas of future urbanization. The language of this change suggests a transition from earlier creations of manicured grounds and monoculture plantings to the establishment of areas resembling the jungle and mangrove native to the island, with wildlife and a greater range of local plants. It marks a desired transition away from constructed nature to regain the forms of 'primitive' nature that were largely lost through Singapore's half-century of urban growth and controlled gardening as guided by the model of the Garden City.

In 1967, when Lee Kuan Yew introduced the idea of the garden city, it was proposed that Singapore would become a garden city by 1970. However, the power of this idea, and its ability to enter other areas of national planning – framing modernization and economic development, guiding national identity and international promotion, and reforming citizens' behaviours – proved to have a much more lasting effect. Instead of a three-year plan, the Garden City became a framework for urban and social planning for more than five decades. Developing from the failed tree planting campaign of 1963, it was re-introduced to find popular success in the 1970s. It entered a new phase in the 1980s, before taking over the entire island of Singapore, at which point the garden city became the 'city in a garden' in 1998. From this point it established an idea of the garden as a nation-wide structure that shaped the city. This model began to absorb its own criticism, and transformed again into the 'city in nature' policy, which plans to conserve and restore a natural environment that has long been lost to urban and economic growth, which only further cements the idea of the garden within the national framework of Singaporeans. Even though the Garden City is now a historical policy, it continues to define Singapore's approach to the development of the urban environment and its ideas of national identity. It made greenery an element of political discourse, a measure of the success of campaigns for societal reform, and a yardstick by which to evaluate the political success of Singapore's government in transforming its physical and social environment.

REFERENCES

[1] See Jesse O'Neill, 'Clean and Disciplined: The Garden City in Singapore', in *The Culture of Nature in the History of Design*, ed. by Kjetil Fallan (London & New York: Routledge, 2019), pp. 89–102.
[2] For example, Belinda Yuen, 'Creating the Garden City: The Singapore Experience', *Urban Studies*, 33:6 (1996), pp. 955–970; Shirlena Huang, 'Planning for a Tropical City of Excellence: Urban Development Challenges for Singapore in the 21st Century', *Built Environment*, 27:2 (2001), pp. 112–128; Heejin Han, 'Singapore, a Garden City', *The Journal of Environment and Development*, 26:1 (2017), pp. 3–24.
[3] Lee Kuan Yew, *The Papers of Lee Kuan Yew: Speeches, Interviews and Dialogues*, 10 vols (Singapore: Cengage Learning Asia, 2012), iv (2012) p. 83.
[4] 'Wah Garden City', *Singapore Free Press and Mercantile Advertiser*, 24 January 1923, p. 53.
[5] '"Plant a Tree" Drive in S'pore', *Straits Times*, 12 June 1963, p. 9.
[6] 'Lee Begins the Tree Campaign', *Straits Times*, 17 June 1963, p. 7.
[7] Timothy P. Barnard and Corinne Heng, 'A City in a Garden', in *Nature Contained: Environmental Histories of Singapore*, ed. by Timothy P. Barnard (Singapore: NUS Press, 2014), pp. 281–306 (p.297).
[8] '"Plant a Tree" Drive in S'pore', *Straits Times*, 12 June 1963, p. 9. 'They Bring Rain Too, Says Minister Wok', *Straits Times*, 3 February 1964, p. 11.
[9] Brenda S.A. Yeoh, *Contesting Space in Colonial Singapore: Power Relations and the Urban Built Environment* (Singapore: NUS Press, 2003), pp. 178–181.
[10] 'Three Ministers Lead the Tree Planters', *Straits Times*, 9 March 1964, p. 5.
[11] 'Body to Make People Care for Trees', *Straits Times*, 19 April 1967, p. 13.
[12] 'Fences', *Straits Times*, 5 September 1967, p. 10.
[13] Nigel P. Taylor, 'The Environmental Relevance of the Singapore Botanic Gardens', in *Nature Contained*, ed. by Barnard, pp. 115–137 (p. 133).
[14] 'Floral Way', *Straits Times*, 21 December 1967, p. 12.
[15] Taylor, p.133.
[16] 'People Ask for Water, They get Trees: MP', *Straits Times*, 20 December 1967, p. 4.
[17] 'Roadside Trees – The Ideal or Practical?', *Straits Times*, 3 December 1965, p. 12.
[18] 'Potongan Cukai P'dapatan Bagi yg Tanam Bunga', *Berita Harian*, 17 February 1973, p. 5.
[19] 'Estate's Clean Up Drive', *Straits Times*, 9 September 1967, p. 5.
[20] 'Teachers Urged to Instil Love for Nature in Students', *Straits Times*, 24 November 1971, p. 12.
[21] Barnard and Heng, p.290.
[22] '20,000 Anak Pokok Akan Ditanam', *Berita Harian*, 24 October 1975, p. 5. 'Hari Tanam Pokok', *Berita Harian*, 7 November 1977, p. 4.
[23] Goh Hong Yi, 'The Nature Society: Endangered Species and Conservation in Singapore', in *Nature Contained*, ed. by Barnard, pp. 245–273 (p. 245).
[24] Lily Kong and Brenda S.A. Yeoh, *The Politics of Landscapes in Singapore: Construction of 'Nation'* (Syracuse: Syracuse University Press, 2003), p. 32.
[25] Barnard and Heng, p. 297.
[26] 'Kempen Kenalkan S'pura kpd Rakyat Jepun Mencapai Kejayaan', *Berita Harian*, 5 October 1974, p. 7.
[27] 'Perlunya Bersikap Lebih Memilih Untuk Berkempen', *Berita Harian*, 17 November 1979, p. 4.
[28] Chris Hudson, *Beyond the Singapore Girl: Discourses of Gender and Nation in Singapore* (Copenhagen: NIAS Press, 2013), p. 18.
[29] Barnard and Heng, p. 295.
[30] *Peltophorum pterocarpum, Cordyline australis, Lagerstroemeria speciosa* and *Erythrina variegata* respectively
[31] Barnard and Heng, p. 291.
[32] Taylor, p. 133.
[33] Gretchen Mahbubani, 'Shaping the Future City', *New Nation*, 7 December 1980, p. 21.
[34] See Goh, pp. 245–273.
[35] 'Green, Blue and Great!', *Straits Times*, 13 September 1991, p. 26.
[36] '"City in a Garden" Plan Set Out for Singapore', *Straits Times*, 11 December 1998.
[37] 'Natural Spaces are Better than Gardens', *Straits Times*, 14 December 1998.
[38] '"City in a Garden": More Greenery for a Healthy Urban Lifestyle', *Today*, 21 October 2002, p. 1.
[39] 'Towards a City in a Garden', *Today*, 26 January 2005, p. 2.
[40] 'Green Cover Count Should Exclude Man-made Spaces', *Today*, 10 November 2015.

THE (INADVERTENT) GREENING OF DETROIT

MICHAEL ANN MULLEN

ABSTRACT

This paper describes crumbling, post-industrial Detroit in the early 2000s and explores the urban farming movement that took root on land left vacant as business and people left the city. Natural vegetation grew on the land as houses and other buildings emptied, were neglected, became dilapidated and eventually fell or were knocked down. The paper explores initiatives started by individuals and groups who cultivated and planted on the derelict land creating productive gardens and farms. It discusses their aims, the success they have achieved and some of the problems they face. A dynamic urban farming movement has grown from these beginnings.

INTRODUCTION

> 'Detroit has been described by some as a ghost town. Parts of the city are so abandoned they have been described as looking like farmland, urban prairie, and even complete wilderness.'

So wrote Rebecca Solnit in 2007.[1] Detroit's population had reached over 1.8 million in 1950 but by 2007 it had fallen to under 850,000 as automobile companies, the economic mainstay, closed one factory after another and jobs vanished. By 2020 the population had recovered slightly but still stood 65 per cent lower than in 1950 and almost a third was living below the poverty line.[2]

Figure 1: A man walks along the pavement of a street near Food Field, an urban farm on the three-acre site of a former primary school and close to the historic Boston Edison District, Detroit. Photo: Michael Ann Mullen (August 2018)

In 2013, when Detroit's emergency financial manager Kevyn Orr filed for Chapter 9 Bankruptcy, there were approximately 78,000 abandoned buildings and up to a third of the land was vacant.[3] In many areas, only a few houses stood in a landscape of weeds and the changing traffic lights surveyed empty streets (Figure 1). What were the city authorities to do with so much vacant land? This paper explores the burgeoning urban farming movement that took root in Detroit in the early 2000s.

URBAN AGRICULTURE ORDINANCE

In the early 2000s vegetable patches, market gardens and small urban farms were being established on vacant land in Detroit. You could cultivate and plant on an abandoned lot, no one would stop you. By 2009, when a senior planner on the Detroit City Planning Commission convened a group of local farmers and market gardeners to formulate an urban agricultural ordinance that would regularize the situation of farms in the city so that they complied with Michigan State law, individuals, community and church groups, educational and charitable organizations, entrepreneurs and businesses were all growing food on land that was vacant, many without knowing who owned it – trespassing in fact. When the Urban Agriculture Ordinance was adopted in 2013, many of the over 1,400 farms and market gardens in operation were also breaking zoning regulations that made it illegal to farm in the city. The land was zoned residential, commercial or industrial, not agricultural.[4]

The Ordinance permits agricultural activity 'to some degree' in all four of the city's land use categories - residential, business, industrial and special and overlay districts - and provides a framework within which urban agriculture enterprises can operate.[5] It prohibits keeping certain farm animals, growing certain species of trees and the cultivation of 'oats, wheat and rye (in order to prevent rodents) except when used as a winter cover crop and not grown to full maturity'. All farming that was going on at the time the Ordinance was adopted was 'deemed conforming' - that is, it was considered legal.[6] This was a very pragmatic way to approach an extraordinary situation.

Establishing a legal framework has encouraged younger people to see a future for farming in the city and given rise to new initiatives. Jack van Dyke and Caroline Ledley bought a house and a lot in the Farnsworth area in 2011 with the intention of farming a small holding. They paid about $5,000 for the house in exchange for paying off back taxes and in 2014 got a $10,000 grant from the Southeast Michigan New Economy Initiative to help install a radiant heating system in their greenhouse.[7] By 2020 their Rising Pheasant Farm extended to half an acre. The heated greenhouse and a bigger, non-heated one added in 2016 make it possible to produce twelve months a year.[8]

The couple, like many other farmers in Detroit, run a Community Supported Agriculture (CSA) scheme. This is a partnership between the farmer and the consumer in which the risks and rewards of the farm are shared. Scheme members pay an amount to the farm each year and in return are allocated a certain amount of produce each week during the growing season. Every farm adjusts the particulars of the scheme to its own circumstances.[9] As well as producing for the CSA scheme, van Dyke and Ledley supply some restaurants and sell produce at Detroit's central Eastern Market and from their own stand once a week.

Another example of a new initiative is Fisheye Farms started by Andy Chase and Amy Eckert in 2015 on a large lot next to a dry cleaners near East Village. In 2018, with a loan from Stewart Investment Trust, the two bought nine lots (0.89 acres in total) in Detroit's Core City neighbourhood near the city centre, where they have a large hoop-house [polytunnel]. The business is based there now but they still grow herbs and flowers on the original lot.[10]

THE FOOD PROBLEM

As Detroit's population declined, businesses including grocery stores closed, creating what have become known as food deserts (Figure 2). The gas stations, convenience and liquor stores that remained sold no fresh produce. In a city with high levels of poverty nearly a quarter of households did not own a car. That, combined with the fact there was almost no public transport, meant that in large areas people were left with few options for accessing fresh food. A 2007 report, 'Examining the Impact of Food Deserts on Public Health in Detroit', concluded that:

> in Detroit a fundamental underpinning of poor nutrition is the dearth of retail outlets that sell a range of nutritious foods at reasonable prices. Fast food and other fringe food outlets are everywhere, yet there are comparatively few quality grocery stores where fresh and healthy foods can be purchased. Particularly striking is the evidence concerning USDA [United States Department of Agriculture] Food Stamp retail patterns. The idea behind the original Food Stamp program was that poor families could use their Food Stamp allocation to acquire the ingredients of a decent diet. In Detroit, however, the Food Stamp program consists primarily of fringe retailers like liquor stores, gas stations, and convenience stores whose range of food offerings is limited and dominated by products that are blatantly bad for your health.[11]

Figure 2: Closed stores in Detroit. Photo: Michael Ann Mullen (July 2014)

Although matters had improved by 2017, with seventy-four full-line grocery stores operating in the city, the Detroit Food Council estimated that 30,000 Detroiters still lacked access to a grocery store that sold fresh produce, meat, fish and dairy products.[12] Around 42 per cent of the population received food stamps and were more likely to access food from fringe retailers.[13] The need to access fresh produce and ensure food security motivated and continues to motivate Detroit's urban agriculture movement.

FARMS, GARDENS and VEGETABLE PLOTS

Farms, market gardens, vegetable patches, flower and nursery gardens, fish farms and a tree farm now occupy land once occupied by houses, stores, cafes, gas stations, schools, libraries, offices and factories. Each has its own aims and objectives but all share crucial concerns about land ownership and financial viability. This section will explore several urban farming initiatives. They are usually called *farms* if over one acre in size and often called *gardens* if smaller.

Hope Takes Root is a community organic garden of about one acre in Corktown, one of the city's oldest residential areas, just west of the commercial centre. It has occupied the present site since 2002. Five members own the land and any expenses are shared. Members of the local community are welcome to volunteer on the site and share the produce.

In 2018, the Ford Motor Company bought the huge, iconic (and derelict) Michigan Central [Railway] Station building nearby and is spending nearly $740 million to transform it and the surrounding area into a tech campus to develop self-drive vehicles.[14] The Ford project is expected to create up to 5,000 jobs and will generate spin-off businesses in the area; the price of housing and land started to rise as soon as the project was announced. Not long after Ford's announcement, the Detroit Planning and Development Department launched the Greater Corktown Planning Framework Study to engage residents in the creation of an area plan. Greening initiatives, including urban farming, community gardens and the development of green infrastructure are central to it.[15] Rejuvenation of the area will have repercussions for Hope Takes Root and for Brother Nature Produce, another farming initiative nearby.

Greg Willerer started ***Brother Nature Farm*** in 2008; a year later he quit his teaching job to work on the farm full time. Now he and Olivia Hubert, his wife, make a living supplying salad crops to local restaurants and selling at Detroit's Eastern Market (Figure 3). According to Willerer, 85 per cent of the original housing stock in his section of Corktown has vanished since the neighbourhood's post-war heyday.[16] Their nearly two-acre farm occupies a square block. They own five parcels of the land and have been trying to buy the other ten for nearly ten years. In autumn 2022, the Detroit Land Bank finally agreed to the sale but because the deal is for so many lots, Brother Nature must wait for City Council approval.[17]

Figure 3: Brother Nature Produce stand at Detroit's Eastern Market. The notice on the smaller board to left of the customer reads 'Food Miles = 1.5' Photo: Michael Ann Mullen (July 2016).

Needing more land over the years and worried they might be evicted if the city found a more lucrative tenant, Willerer and Hubert have bought land in New Haven, about forty miles north east. The additional land gives them the capacity to supply all their restaurant customers. Committed to environment-friendly food production and to making Detroit a food-sovereign city Willerer and Hubert attribute the farm's success to the freshness of their produce and their willingness to deliver several times a week if necessary to the small restaurants they supply.[18]

In east Detroit the Capuchin Monastery of St Joseph runs a soup kitchen. It was started in 1929 to feed unemployed workers and their families during the Great Depression. The Soup Kitchen started a garden in the late 1990s and this has grown into ***Earthworks Urban Farm***, a one-and-a-quarter-acre certified organic farm.[19] The twenty lots it occupies lie within a two-block radius and are owned by the Soup Kitchen. In previous times houses stood on most of this land. 'The farm was created to connect people to each other, the land and their food' explains the Earthworks website.[20] Work is done by volunteers and the growing programme runs from February to December.

The farm's output supplies the Monastery's two soup kitchens, is sold at its Meldrum Fresh Market, and distributed to volunteers when there is enough. Some is also donated to Gleaners Food Bank nearby. Earthworks also sells honey from its apiary, makes and sells its own jams and produces transplants for thousands of community gardens. These are distributed through Keep Growing Detroit's Garden Resource Program, discussed below. Earthworks employs a manager and assistant manager, as well as an education coordinator and a programme manager. Like many of Detroit's community farming initiatives, they run educational and training programmes for the local community.

D-Town Farm, a seven-acre organic farm run by the Detroit Black Community Food Security Network (DBCFSN), moved to its present site in River Rouge Park on Detroit's West side in 2008. The site is owned by the City of Detroit and was once the home of the Meyers Tree Nursery which provided trees for Detroit's streets and parks. The farm, which generates a small amount of electricity from solar panels, produces vegetables, fruit and honey with the help of individuals and groups of volunteers, trainees and a small number of paid staff. The produce is sold from a stall on the site on Saturday and Sunday morning and at several farmers' markets (Figure 4). Wholesale discounts are available to stores, caterers and restaurants.

Figure 4: Saturday Food stand at D-Town Farm. Photo: Michael Ann Mullen (August 2018).

Farming is part of DBCFSN's commitment to building food security in Detroit's Black community. Founded by Malik Yakini, its aim is to ensure that Detroit's African-American population participate in the food movement and, because they comprise over 80 percent of the population, to ensure that they are in the leadership of that movement locally.[21] The organization headed the initiative for the City Council to adopt a Food Security Policy in March 2008 and director Malik Yakini was the first chair of the Detroit Food Policy Council set up the next year.[22] Volunteers learn agricultural skills and D-Town runs educational programmes for the local community and a twelve-week full-time summer training programme for ten interns when funding allows.

D-Town and Earthworks are among the many Detroit food producers explicitly committed to the principles of the US Food Justice and the International Food Sovereignty Movements.[23] These movements are committed to creating sustainable, environmentally friendly and socially just alternatives to the industrialized and socially unequal food system that dominates the west. Small plots of land where individuals or small groups can produce their own food are integral to this vision and Detroit has an abundance of these. Both D-Town and Earthworks work closely with Keep Growing Detroit, a non-profit organization started in 2013. Its mission is to promote a food sovereign city where the majority of fruits and vegetables consumed by Detroiters are grown by residents within the city's limits.[24] The organization maintains that by using just 5,000 acres for farming, Detroit could become almost self-sufficient in fresh fruit and vegetables. There are no figures for how much land was in food production in 2022.

The ***Michigan Urban Farming Initiative*** was started in 2012 by two University of Michigan students when they bought a derelict six-unit apartment building close to the downtown area. Their aim was to create an urban farm on the derelict land (that they did not own) across the street and use the building as its headquarters. The farm has acquired several more derelict buildings since – the basement of one was converted into a cistern to harvest rainwater for the farm's irrigation system, the others were torn down to expand the growing area to three acres (Figure 5). In 2018, after protracted negotiations with the Detroit Land Bank, they were able to buy eight of the lots they were already farming.[25] The farm work is done by volunteers - most from outside the neighbourhood.

Figure 5: Michigan Urban Farming Initiative (MUFI) vegetable field. Photo: Michael Ann Mullen (July 2015)

MUFI sells produce to a number of local restaurants and donates to a local church and two food pantries. However, at its Saturday Market Stall, produce is given away: farm manager Tyrone Garth thinks the returns are too low to justify selling it. This practice is condemned by other community-based farming initiatives as 'neo-colonial', encouraging a dependence culture. It also undermines the urban farming sector's effort to become self-supporting. Detroit-born Jerry Hebron, from ***Oakland Avenue Farm*** nearby, concedes that 'it's tough to make money', but highlights one of the positives of doing so: her five-and-a-half-acre farm provides thirteen full and part-time jobs. It is a place where those with employment barriers go to learn skills and build a resumé before moving on to bigger things.[26]

However, for MUFI's Tyrone Garth the focus is on using the farm's resources to develop 'America's First Sustainable Urban Agrihood.' *Agrihood* is a recently-coined term used to describe master-planned housing communities focused around working farms. They are expensive private developments built on large sites in suburbs or rural areas, and target well-off buyers. Garth describes MUFI's *agrihood* as 'a diverse agricultural campus that aims to help sustain the neighbourhood and attract new residents and investment into the area'.[27] The rising land values created by the presence of a working farm and his failure to consult appropriately with the existing local community are contentious issues: MUFI's Urban Agrihood prioritizes the creation of an environment ripe for middle class development over the needs of the surrounding community which is predominantly black and working class.

Located not far away, ***Georgia Street Community Garden*** was started by Mark Covington in 2007. Unlike MUFI, it is a grassroots initiative in a neighbourhood once filled with homes for well-paid blue-collar workers, but now peppered with vacant lots and derelict houses. In an effort to stop persistent dumping on vacant land near his grandmother's home, Mark started clearing and mowing, but dumping continued. It was not until he had cultivated and planted the lots with vegetables that dumping stopped. Neighbours joined in to help with clearing and planting but no one knew much about farming. Chance contact with the Garden Resources Program run by Keep Growing Detroit provided access to information and training and to a network of other growers. Following the creation of the Georgia Street Community Collective in 2008 the project expanded to include a composting area, an orchard, bee hives, poultry, pigs and goats. After a long battle with the Detroit Land Bank to buy them, Georgia Street Community Collective now owns seventeen of the lots it works on.[28]

By summer 2018 the focus of the project had changed from community farming to beautification of the area and community building. The farm produces vegetables, fruit, honey and eggs. Most of the work is done by volunteers from outside the area –'school and university students and repair-the-world community service type people', says Covington.[29] Why has the community's involvement in farming diminished? Covington does not know. Countering this, the project's after-school homework labs are well attended and local teachers rate them highly.

Hantz Woodlands, probably the most controversial agricultural venture in present-day Detroit, is a tree farm of around 140 acres owned by John Hantz, a local businessman. Midst angry controversy and after long deliberation, the City Council agreed to sell Hantz around 1,500 vacant lots for $500,000 in 2013 – the City had acquired most of this land as a result of tax default. The lots lie within one square mile.[30] This is not a tree farm in the traditional sense. The trees are planted in rows on non-contiguous lots around inhabited and derelict houses dotted along a grid of city streets (Figure 6).

Figure 6: Saplings planted in rows, Hantz Woodlands, Detroit. Photo: Michael Ann Mullen (July 2016).

Fifteen thousand saplings were planted on twenty acres in May 2014 by 1,000 volunteers. By 2022 more than 36,000 trees had been planted.[31] Hardwoods are being used, mostly oak and maple, because the local community objected to the fruit trees Hantz first proposed. These would have required large-scale spraying and created a serious health hazard for the area's inhabitants.

John Hantz views the Woodlands project as investment in the city. He paid cash for land and is clearing derelict houses from the site. The project mows the grass every ten to fourteen days during the growing season, maintaining the area at its own expense, and has invested heavily in removing dangerous structures.[32] Many of Detroit's farming initiatives are community based and receive funding from charities. Hantz proudly points out that his is a commercial enterprise that aims to make a profit as well as to beautify and improve the area.[33] Many view this initiative as a land grab.[34]

At the other end of the scale from commercial and non-profit initiatives are countless ***individuals*** planting and harvesting for themselves, their families and their immediate communities. In the early days, some owned and others did not know who owned the land they were working on.

A good example is Arthur Mullen who started his Vernor Charlevoix Community Garden in 2009 on derelict land where houses once stood. The garden lies across an alley that defines the boundary between the City of Detroit and the largely upper-middle class suburb of Grosse Pointe where Arthur lives. 'I wanted to build a visual bridge across the border and connect with Detroiters', he explains. 'I hoped that working together on the garden would help break down some of the preconceived ideas that people in Detroit and Grosse Pointe have about one another'. 'Please take what you will use' says a board by the garden. Not many people do. Mullen feels that the aims of the project have morphed: 'I feel like the garden is my part of Detroit and I try to maintain it as well as I can, clear trash off the site, cut the grass and make it productive and look cared for', says Mullen.[35] He grows vegetables, strawberries and blueberries and picks wild raspberries from bushes he transplanted nearby. The land is owned by the Detroit City Land Bank. After cultivating it for over ten years he applied to buy it. His application was refused: the reason given, he 'was not an adjacent City of Detroit resident'.[36]

THE RESPONSE OF THE CITY AUTHORITIES

What was the city to do with all the land that had become vacant by the early twenty-first century was the question asked at the start of this paper. In 2010 the then mayor Dave Bing set up the Detroit Works Project, a two-year community consultation and fact-finding initiative, to address this question.[37] The project began as an effort to deal with the increasing amount of land becoming vacant and expanded to look at how land use ties into everything else in the city. 'The 'Detroit Future City Strategic Framework Plan', which devotes 150 pages to 'The Land Use Element,'[38] was released in late 2012. A few months later Detroit declared bankruptcy. There was no time to consider the Strategic Plan and it lay neglected for several years.

While the authorities were occupied with the city's financial collapse, individuals and groups like those discussed here cleared and planted land and began to develop a varied and viable urban agriculture sector. By making farming in the city legal, the Urban Agriculture Ordinance, which was adopted by the City Council in 2013, cleared the way for this kind of development. After coming out of bankruptcy in 2014 and regaining control of its own finances, Detroit started to adopt greening policies. In 2016 the Detroit Works Project was renamed Detroit Future City, restructured and made an independent, non-profit organization. It now operates as a think tank to facilitate implantation of the vision outlined in the Detroit Future City Strategic Framework Plan. In 2017 the Mayor's Office of Sustainability was set up with a Land Based Projects section responsible for projects that use 'land for urban agriculture, gardening, beautification' and other productive purposes. Other greening initiatives include those included in the Greater Corktown Planning Framework mentioned above. However unlike Atlanta, whose Planning Department appointed an Urban Agriculture Director in 2015, and Baltimore whose 'Office of Sustainability' implements Homegrown Baltimore, its urban agriculture plan, Detroit has not yet published an urban agriculture policy or plan.[39]

CONCLUSION

This paper has explored the context for and development of Detroit's urban farming movement. Detroit's prosperity rested on the auto industry. By the early 2000s the majority of the auto factories had closed leaving their sites to become derelict. Many of the workers and businesses that depended on the industry moved away leaving the city with vast areas of empty land. Unplanned, some of the people who remained started to grow food on the vacant areas. By 2022 there were more than 2,029 farms and gardens in the city.[40] They were being run by individuals, families, schools, community groups, market gardeners and businessmen. Exploration of a few has highlighted their aims, organization, scale and some of the problems faced by this kind of unplanned greening.

REFERENCES

[1] Rebecca Solnit, 'Detroit Arcadia: Exploring the post-American landscape.' *Harpers Magazine*, July 2007: https://harpers.org/archive/2007/07/detroit-arcadia [accessed 12/3/21]

[2] US Census Bureau. QuickFacts, Detroit City, Michigan: https://www.census.gov/quickfacts/fact/table/detroitcitymichigan/PST120219 [accessed 23/2/21].

[3] Dominic Rushie, 'Detroit becomes largest US city to file for bankruptcy in historic "low point"'. *The Guardian*, 18 July 2013: https://www.theguardian.com/world/2013/jul/18/detroit-formally-files-bankruptcy [accessed 25/1/23].

[4] J. Hand and Amanda Gregory, 'The Detroit Frontier: Urban Agriculture in a Legal Vacuum', *Chicago-Kent Law Review*, 92:2 (30 October 2017): https://scholarship.kentlaw.iit.edu/cgi/viewcontent.cgi?article=4160&context=cklawreview [accessed 21/2/21].

[5] Kathryn Lynch, 'City of Detroit Urban Agricultural Ordinance Abridged', April 2013: http://www.detroitmi.gov/Portals/0/docs/cpc/pdf/Urban%20Ag%20Ordinance%20Abridged_Apr2013.pdf?ver=2013-04-19-164058-087 [accessed 23/2/21].
[6] Flaminia Paddeu, 'Legalising urban agriculture in Detroit: A contested way of planning for decline', *The Town Planning Review*, 88:1 (January 2017), pp. 109-29 (p.118).
[7] Michael Park, 'Detroit's Small but Mighty Rising Pheasant Farms', *bon appétit,* 29 December 2015: https://www.bonappetit.com/people/out-of-the-kitchen/article/rising-pheasant-farms, [accessed 24/2/21]; John Gallagher, 'NEIdeas announces third round of grants plus bonus year', *Detroit Free Press*, 22 November 2016: https://neweconomyinitiative.org/detroit-free-press-neideas-announces-third-round-of-grants-plus-bonus-year/ [accessed 29/1/23].
[8] Jon Zemke, 'Rising Pheasant Farms grows urban ag operation on east side', *Model D,* 10.2.201: https://www.modeldmedia.com/startupnews/risingpheasantfarmsdetroit021015.aspx [accessed 24/2/21]
[9] Community Supported Agriculture 'What is CSA?': https://communitysupportedagriculture.org.uk/what-is-csa/ [accessed 24/2/21].
[10] Fisheye Farms website, https://fisheyefarms.com, [accessed 24/2/23/].
[11] Mari Gallagher, 'Examining the Impact of Food Deserts on Public Health in Detroit', Mari Gallagher Research and Consulting Group, https://www.marigallagher.com/2007/06/19/examining-the-impact-of-food-deserts-on-public-health-in-detroit-june-19-2007/ [accessed 24/2/21].
[12] Jerilyn Jordon, 'New report reveals 30,000 Detroiters do not have access to healthy food', *Detroit Metro Times*, 8 March 2018; https://www.metrotimes.com/news-hits/archives/2018/03/08/new-report-reveals-30000-detroiters-do-not-have-access-to-healthy-food [accessed 24/2/21].
[13] Statistical Atlas website, 2020. *Food Stamps in Detroit, Michigan.* Website owned by Cedar Lake Ventures, Minneapolis: https://statisticalatlas.com/place/Michigan/Detroit/Food-Stamps [accessed 24/2/21].
[14] Cindy Burton, 'Ford says it will spend $740M to bring Detroit train station project to life', *Detroit Free Press,* 15 August 2018: https://eu.freep.com/story/money/business/2018/08/15/michigan-central-station-corktown-cost-740-million/994867002/ [accessed 24/2/21].
[15] HR&A Advisors, 'Greater Corktown Neighborhood Framework and Choice Implementation', 2023: https://www.hraadvisotrs.com/portfolio/greater-corktown/ [accessed 7/3/23].
[16] Tom Philpott, 'Three projects that are watering Detroit's "food desert"', *Grist,* 11 September 2010: https://grist.org/article/food-three-projects-that-are-watering-detroits-food-desert/ [accessed 24/2/21].
[17] Jena Brooker, 'After a decade, Corktown farm could own its own land', *Bridge Detroit,* 25 October 2022: https://www.bridgedetroit.com/corktown-farm/ [accessed 28/1/23]
[18] Michael Jackman, 'Greg Willerer is cultivating more than lettuce at Brother Nature Produce', *Metro Times,* 25 July 2018: https://www.metrotimes.com/detroit/greg-willerer-brother-nature-produce/Content?oid=14096181 [accessed 24/2/21].
[19] Earthworks Urban Farm. 2020. *Capuchins*: https://www.cskdetroit.org/earthworks/about_us/capuchins/ [accessed 24/2/21].
[20] Earthworks Urban Farm website: 'History', https://www.cskdetroit.org/earthworks/about_us/history/ [accessed 4/1/23].
[21] Detroit Black Food Security Network 2020: https://www.dbcfsn.org [accessed 24/2/21].
[22] Detroit Food Policy Council, 2022: https://www.detroitfoodpc.org [accessed 30/1/23]
[23] For an introduction to the US Food Justice and the International Food Sovereignty Movements see: L. Farthing, and N. Romer, 'Food Justice + Food Sovereignty', *New Politics,* 2016: https://newpol.org/issue_post/food-justice-food-sovereignty/ [accessed 24/2/21].
[24] Keep Growing Detroit, 2020: http://detroitagriculture.net/about/ [accessed 24/2/21].
[25] Christine Macintyre, 'Detroit nonprofit paves the way for innovative urban agriculture', *The Crazy Wisdom Community Journal,* 30 August 2022: https://www.crazywisdomjournal.com/featuredstories/2022/8/30/detroit-nonprofit-paves-the-way-for-innovative-urban-agriculture [accessed: 4/1/23]

[26] Tom Perkins, 'On urban farming and "colonialism" in Detroit's North End neighborhood', *Detroit Metro Times,* 20 December 2017: https://www.metrotimes.com/detroit/on-urban-farming-and-colonialism-in-detroits-north-end-neighborhood/Content?oid=7950059 [accessed 24/2/21].
[27] Biba Adams, 'In Detroit, A New Type of Agricultural Neighborhood Has Emerged' *Yes! Magazine,* 5 November 2019: https://www.yesmagazine.org/social-justice/2019/11/05/food-community-detroit-garden-agriculture/ [accessed 24/2/21].
[28] Nancy Kaffer, 'Does Farming have a place in the new Detroit?', *Detroit Free Press,*6 July 2018: https://eu.freep.com/story/opinion/columnists/nancy-kaffer/2018/07/07/detroit-urban-farming-development/745550002/ [accessed 24/2/21].
[29] Michael Ann Mullen, interview with Mark Covington, August 2018.
[30] David Sands, 'Hantz Woodlands deal approved by Detroit City Council 5-4'. *Huffington Post*, 11 December 2012: https://www.huffingtonpost.co.uk/2012/12/11/hantz-woodlands-deal-detroit-city-council_n_2278440.html [accessed 24/2/21].
[31] Hantz Farms website, 2022. 'What we have done' : https://www.hantzfarmsdetroit.com/whatwehavedone.html [accessed 21.2.23]
[32] Hantz Farms website, 2022. 'What we have done' : https://www.hantzfarmsdetroit.com/whatwehavedone.html [accessed 21.2.23].
[33] Detroit Future City website, 2022, 'Hantz Woodlands': https://detroitfuturecity.com/whatwedo/land-use/DFC-lots/local-examples/hantz-woodlands [accessed 20/2/23].
[34] Hantz Farms website, 2022. 'Our Story'; 'Land Grab' video: https://www.hantzfarmsdetroit.com/ourstory.html [accessed 21/2/23].
[35] Michael Ann Mullen, Interview with Arthur Mullen, August 2018.
[36] Arthur Mullen, email to Michael Ann Mullen, 26 February 2023.
[37] Sarah Cwiek, 'Strategic framework for Detroit's future and $150 million to back it', *Michigan Radio,* 9 January 2013: https://www.michiganradio.org/post/strategic-framework-detroits-future-and-150-million-back-it [accessed 25/2/21].
[38] Detroit Future City, 2012, *Detroit Future City Strategic Framework Plan,* 'The Land Use Element', pp.195-345: https://detroitfuturecity.com/wp-content/uploads/2017/07/DFC_LandUse_2nd.pdf [accessed 25/2/21].
[39] Michael Ann Mullen, 2021, 'Detroit: Farming is re-defining the Urban Landscape'. Available from https://www.academia.edu/46809492/DETROIT_Farming_is_re_defining_an_urban_landscape.
[40] Keep Growing Detroit, 2022 Annual Report, [online - accessed 4/3/23]. Available from: https://static1.squarespace.com/static/61ddad815f23d9286ca6ab1c/t/63dc2c3d7826ad18cb89b9d3/1675373643412/2022_KGD_Annual+Report_Final_Share-compressed.pdf

4

GARDENS, POLITICS AND POWER

Gardens and designed landscapes have been used as symbols of power since antiquity. Mastery of hydraulic engineering, collections of exotic plants and trees and the ability to impose a sense of order on the landscape with earthworks or straight lines have all added to the perceived power of the garden's owner. Conversely, gardens have sometimes been used to express opposition to the policies of those in power, opposition or defiance also finding outlets in garden-related subjects, such as poems or essays. On occasion opposition has even found expression in the destruction of the very gardens that were the totems of a ruler or ruling faction. This chapter elaborates on some of these aspects as it explores the use of 'garden power' at roughly the same point in time but on two different continents.

In Mexico, the Aztecs' rise to power was primarily a matter of force, but their sustained domination of the Valley of Mexico and beyond in the fifteenth century also owed much to their agricultural and horticultural prowess. From their former Tepanec overlords they had learned the political value of beautiful gardens and cities, and they filled their own with exotic plants demanded, in a further display of power, as tribute from people under their dominion. Although profoundly impressed by the Aztec elite's gardens, the Spanish invaders saw fit to destroy them during the conquest of Mexico in 1519-1521.

Less than forty years later, in 1556, Philip II acceded to the Spanish throne and embarked on an ambitious programme of garden-building around Madrid designed to enhance the city's status as the country's new capital. The second paper in this chapter studies Philip's project at Aranjuez, one of the many projects around Madrid, and one which points up the monarch's strong Burgundian heritage. Given that the Burgundian realm had always been made up of many disparate territories, its rulers, Valois and Habsburg, faced a particular challenge of creating a sense of unity and emphasizing their own authority. Gardens and, equally importantly, representations of gardens in many forms were part of their strategy.

CULTIVATING POWER, PROGRESS AND POSTERITY IN AZTEC MEXICO

JEANNE GILLESPIE

ABSTRACT

This study examines colonial Spanish and Nahuatl[1] documents recounting the migration of the Mexica people who would eventually form the principal city or *altepetl* of the Aztec Empire. As they sought an appropriate site for their own city, they learned agricultural and horticultural techniques that helped them feed their growing population. These techniques and others that they would develop to survive in the brackish waters of Lake Texcoco also provided the Mexica with the skills necessary to appease local overlords and to eventually create luxurious garden palaces designed for their own pleasure and to impress their vassals and adversaries.

AN ELITE AZTEC GARDEN IN THE VALLEY OF MEXICO

When the Spanish conquistadors arrived in the Valley of Mexico they were astounded by the magnificence of the Aztec leaders' gardens. They were supposed to be. These gardens were created not just for pleasure and relaxation but, filled as they were with exotic plants, waterworks, animals and precious stones, designed to leave a clear impression of power and wealth on visitors.

Coming from the Gulf of Mexico Hernán Cortés and his troops reached Itzapalapa in the autumn of 1519. Located at the base of an extinct volcano, on the peninsula of the same name, Iztapalapa was an important waystation guarding the entrance to the causeway linking it to the capital (or *huey altepetl* in Nahuatl) Tenochtitlan (Figure 1). Considering its strategic position it is not surprising that the supreme ruler (*huey tlatoani*), Moctezuma II (c. 1466-1520), had appointed his younger brother, Cuitláhuac, to be its ruler or that the latter should have a fine palace (*huey tecpan* - grand noble's palace). It was here that he entertained the leaders of Cortés's expedition.

A letter that Cortés sent to the King of Spain, Charles V, the Holy Roman Emperor and King of Spain (r. 1519-1556), shows just how impressive the Cuitláhuac's *huey tecpan* was:

> [t]here are ... very refreshing gardens with many trees and sweet-scented flowers, well-constructed pools of fresh water with steps leading to the bottom. Near the house with many beautiful corridors and rooms [there is also] a large orchard. [The house is] overlooked by a high terrace. Within the orchard is a great square pool of fresh water, very well-constructed, with sides of attractive masonry, around which runs a walk with a well-laid pavement of tiles, so wide that four persons can walk abreast on it, and 400 paces square, making in all 1,600 paces. On the other side of this promenade toward the wall of the garden are hedges of lattice work made of cane, behind [these] are all sorts of plantations of trees and aromatic herbs. The pool contains many fish and different kinds of waterfowl.[2]

For Bernal Díaz del Castillo, Cortés's aide, the *huey tecpan* and its surroundings at Iztapalapa were more impressive than anything he had seen before or that he could have imagined existed. He described (in Spanish) the orchard and garden as being filled with a great diversity of trees with different scents, and with *andenes llenos de rosas y flores, y muchos frutales y rosales de la tierra, y un estanque de agua dulce* [platforms full of roses and flowers, and many local fruit trees and rose bushes, and a freshwater pond].[3] Díaz del Castillo's use of the term *andenes* is significant here. In this situation, the term describes promenades or platforms built out from the land into Lake Texcoco. Díaz del Castillo remarks that *era muy gran pueblo, y que estaba poblada la mitad de las casas en tierra y la otra mitad en el agua* [it was a very large city, and it was populated [with] half of the houses on land and the other half in the water].[4] In fact, the name 'Iztapalapa' can be translated as 'built on pavers'.

In the letter he wrote to King Charles, Cortés gave a similar description, saying how the city was 'half in the water and the other half on *terra firma*'.[5] Indeed archaeologist Richard Blanton confirms that Iztapalapa and two other cities on the peninsula, Culhuacan and Mexicaltzingo, 'were constructed wholly or partially on artificial surfaces in the lakes'.[6]

Figure 1. Valley of Mexico c. 1519, from Michael Coe, Dean Snow and Elizabeth Benson, *Atlas of Ancient America* (New York: Facts on File, 1986), p. 240.

REFLECTION OF WATERBORNE INGENUITY – THE MEXICA AND THEIR BORROWINGS

The construction of the lakeside cities out into the water was not the only feat of engineering that impressed the European visitors. The platforms which Díaz del Castillo referred to were also remarkable:

> *Y otra cosa de ver: que podían entrar en el vergel grandes canoas desde la laguna por una abertura que tenían hecha, sin saltar en tierra, e todo muy encalado y lucido, de muchas maneras de piedras e pinturas en ellas, que había harto que ponderar.*
>
> [And another sight to see: that large canoes could enter into the garden from the lake through an opening they had made, without jumping to the ground, all very white-washed and shiny with all sorts of stone, and paintings on them, that there was so much to ponder.][7]

This description of gardens with openings for boats to enter from the lake offers the first mention in Spanish sources of the practice of raised-bed cultivation along the lakeshore known in Nahuatl as *chinampan* (place of the fenced fields). Over the course of centuries, the major cities (*altepemeh*) which emerged there developed a system of *chinampas* or raised fields along the shores of a chain of volcanic lakes that spread through the Valley of Mexico. This practice entailed building long oval fences out into the lakebed and then filling them with muck from the lake bottom, plant debris, and rubble piled several inches above the water level, creating a plot of rich fertile land that needed no irrigation (Figure 2a). This type of plot, called a *chinamitl* (fenced field), would survive even severe drought. In Spanish 'chinampan' became *chinampa*, and the term *chinamperos* referred to the local farmers who cultivated these plots. This technique is still an active method of cultivation.

Figure 2: Model of *chinampa* construction (a) with *ahuejotes* (*Salix bonplandiana*) planted along the sides of the *chinamitl* for support (b); also (c) showing a model of the *semillero* (seed starter bed) technology. Model from the Museo del Templo Mayor, Mexico DF. Photo and annotations by author.

When the Mexica (who would eventually emerge in the fourteenth century as the most powerful force in the Aztec Triple Alliance)[8] first settled on the Iztapalapa Peninsula in the twelfth century, chinampa construction was already well-established along the length of the southern shore of the fresh water lakes Xochimilco and Chalco.[9] The Mexica remained in the region until the early part of the thirteenth century when they clashed with their neighbours and migrated north to the city of Tula and later resettled for a short time on the island of Xaltocan in Lake Xaltocan. Here they discovered that, if they filled in the enclosures with fresh soil brought from the shore and planted crops with shallow enough roots, they could deploy the chinampa cultivation technique they had learned in the southern valley, even in the brackish water of the northern Lake Texcoco.[10]

The Mexica continued to wander through the Valley of Mexico (Figure 3), eventually concentrating their settlements along the western shore of Lake Texcoco where they became vassals of the Azcapotzalcans in the early fourteenth century. Their interactions with these overlords forced them to make further innovations.

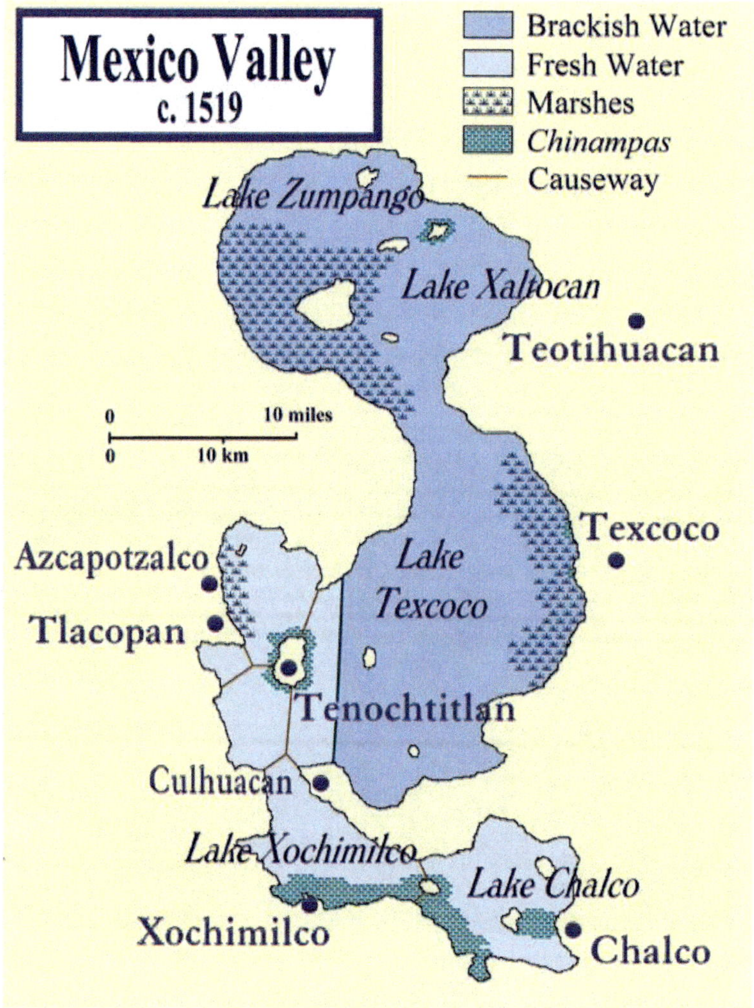

Figure 3: A representation of the chain of lakes in the Basin of Mexico indicating major cities (*altepemeh*), water quality, marshlands and human interventions including a dike, three majors causeways leading from the shore to Tenochtitlan and chinampas. Wikimedia Commons License: CC-BY-SA-3.0

ADAPTING IN THE FACE OF POWER

Under Tepanec rule from Azcapotzalco, the Mexica were forced to develop their horticultural expertise in the face of demands for tribute from the powerful *huey tlatoani*. The tribute consisted initially of food plants, fish, frogs and other lacustrine products that could be cultivated in their chinampas[11] but, in time, the ruler of Azcapotzalco became dissatisfied with their efforts, believing that they were not doing enough to honour him:

> he decided to ask for additional tribute that he believed would be impossible for them to provide. His advisers pointed out that the Mexica paid very little in tribute and that he wanted to increase it and he needed to repair and beautify his city; that together with the tribute that they usually paid they should bring full-grown *ahuehuete* (cypress) and *ahuejote* (willow) trees to plant in his city, and they also would bring a *sementera* (planted bed) that moved itself like a raft across the surface of the lake, and that they would sow seeds in it that they used for his sustenance.[12]

When the Mexica heard of the new tribute demands, it is said that they 'began to cry' but their patron divinity Huitzilopochtli came to one of his followers in the night and instructed the Mexica to bring cypress and willow trees to Azcapotzalco and suggested they should build the raft mentioned above, seeding it with all the plants that the ruler demanded. This they did, bringing the trees they were asked for and also constructing the floating plant bed seeded with 'corn stalks, chile, tomatoes, amaranth, beans, squash and many flowers, all at their peak and in season. The *tlatoani* marvelled over this and told his court that when he had ordered it, he had not believed it possible.'[13] Once the *huey tlatoani* realized the extent of his vassals' horticultural abilities, he demanded even more: the Mexica were to create a new floating tribute raft that would contain, in addition to the required plants, a nesting duck and heron whose chicks would hatch on arrival at Azcapotzalco. They were to do so on pain of death. Apparently, though, this feat was also achieved, thanks again to advice from their god – and to the great admiration of the *tlatoani*.[14] Rafts are still used today to transport plants (Figure 4).

Figure 4: *Chinamperos* transporting plants by raft. Photo: courtesy of United Nations Food and Agriculture Organization.

Another way that the Mexica found to help themselves was through the cultivation and distribution of starter plants. They developed a system of seed starter beds and then used the rafts they had designed for their tribute payments, enabling them to easily deliver the starter plants to markets throughout the valley. Archaeologist Zelia Nuttall (1857-1933) described the *semilleros* (seed starter beds) and the *sementeras movedizas* (movable planted beds) for transport thus:

> The sale of starter plants also constituted an important enterprise, and they were obtained in a very unique way: within a fence, upon a substratum of already decomposed aquatic plants, they spread a cap of liquid mud from 6 to 7 inches thick, which was allowed to dry out. The plants would be placed in the *semillero* at equal distances throughout the bed, and when they had sent out roots and grown, [the chinampaneros] would water the plot well and divide it into smaller equal blocks, cutting the mud with a knife. When each cube of earth was almost dry, with its respective plant, whose roots had developed perfectly, they would be able to be to lift, handle, and transport them easily. Once planted in the gardens, the plants would develop rapidly.[15]

While chinampas tended to rise just two or three inches above the water's surface, these seed starter constructions consisted of an extra six to seven inches of liquid mud, which gave the plants in the *semilleros* room to develop roots and allowed them to be planted in the *chinamitl* at the ideal depth (Figure 2c).

The Mexicas' ability successfully to deliver the tribute demanded by their overlords derived not just from their ingenuity with seed starters and planted rafts but also from fertilizing techniques. With sophisticated cycles of crop rotation, chinampas produced multiple crops per year which required that the nutritive value of the soil be maintained. The Mexica devised a system to keep their cities clean and to have a supply of manure and urea available to support their intensive agricultural and horticultural needs. Katherine Ashenberg explains the practice in Tenochtitlan:

> At a time in Europe when street cleaning was almost non-existent and people emptied their overflowing chamber pots into the streets as a matter of course, the Aztecs employed a thousand public service cleaners to sweep and water their streets daily, built public toilets in every neighbourhood, and transported human waste in canoes for use as fertilizer.[16]

With this knowledge, the *tlatoani* Cuitláhuac's name – translated as 'excrement in the water' – takes on a special and positive meaning. In fact, ordure was so prized that the Aztecs called the mineral gold *teocuicatl* (divine excrement) and silver *iztac teocuicatl* (white divine excrement).

AGRICULTURAL AND HORTICULTURAL RUNGS TO POWER

Apart from their military strength, the Aztec/Mexicas' agricultural prowess proved to be an important factor in their rise to power. During the fifteenth century, they subjugated former allies and overlords and extended their dominion across most of what we now know as Mexico. Through their knowledge and expertise in agriculture, they were able to maintain a burgeoning population. In 1519, when the

Europeans arrived in Anahuac, the south-central area of the Valley of Mexico, their agricultural practices were feeding at least a million people. The population of the city of Tenochtitlan was at least 350,000 and Iztapalapa had between 10,000 and 15,000 inhabitants.[17]

Horticulture was a powerful tool in the Aztec's political armoury too. Just as the ruler of Azcapotzalco had known that beautifying his city would enhance the prestige he was held in and the power he wielded, so the new Aztec leaders and elite created elaborate gardens which, as already mentioned, were not just for retreat and recreation but also settings for political events. The gardens created by Netzahualcoyotl (1402-1472), the powerful leader of Texcoco, on and around Chapultepec and at Texcotzingo are outstanding examples; so too those of Moctezuma I (1440-1469) near Huastepec. When the Spaniards arrived there were royal gardens not just at Chapultepec, Texcoco and Huastepec but others in Tenochtitlan, el Peñon and, as already noted, Itzapalapa.[18]

As well as installing impressive water features such as the large pond at Iztapalapa, the Aztec leaders greatly expanded the range of plants cultivated in their gardens, using the tribute system to demand that new species be brought from vassal peoples in other parts of the realm. As Patricia Granziera has noted, these plants themselves were proclamations of the 'extent of the empire and the power of the ruling class'.[19]

AFTERLIFE

Cuitláhuac, whose name and productive city expressed the power and aesthetic of the Aztec nation, succeeded his brother Moctezuma II after the latter was murdered in Spanish custody, but reigned for only eighty days, succumbing to the smallpox epidemic that ravaged the valley with the introduction of European pathogens. His city, Iztapalapa, was the first to be destroyed by the Europeans and their indigenous allies, because of its strategic access to the causeway. Díaz del Castillo wrote of the devastation of Iztapalapa that 'today all that I then saw is overthrown and destroyed: nothing is left standing'.[20] Other garden palaces throughout the empire, including Chapultepec, Texcotzingo, and Huastepec were systematically destroyed because they were designed to convey the tremendous power of the Aztec state. In 1920 Zelia Nuttall lamented the deliberate destruction of many of the great Aztec gardens:

> I am sure that every lover of botany and horticulture will share the sadness that I feel after remembering the beauty of the gardens of ancient Mexico now disappeared, the ones that ... shared so many delights with generations of ancient Mexicans who were such lovers of gardening and flowers.[21]

However, there are still reminders of the Aztecs' horticultural skills and glory 500 years on, including the willow and cypress trees which the *tlatoani* of Azcapotzalco had demanded the Mexica provide in tribute. The *ahuejotes* (*Salix bonplandiana,* Bonpland willow), are fast-growing trees that love the water. The *chinamperos* used to weave their long roots into the chinampas for stability and support while also cutting back their branches so that the plots would receive the sunlight needed to thrive (Figure 2b) They also used *ahuejotes* to tether the floating beds until they were ready to be used as transport. *Ahuejotes* still thrive in the chinampas of Xochimilco (Figure 5).

The *ahuehuete*, specifically *Taxodium mucronatum* or Montezuma bald cypress, is a slow- growing, water-loving tree that lives for hundreds of years. Its name means 'old man of the water'

Figure 5. Chinampa with mature *ahuehuetes* in Xochimilco in the Basin of Mexico.
Photo: Eneas de Troya, Creative Commons 2.0

and over the years these trees have been planted as monuments of strength and power. Many of them still survive throughout Mexico. In fact, one of the massive *ahuehuetes* in the city of Azcapotzalco near the church of Santa Catarina was probably planted during the city-scaping project that resulted from the products of Mexica tribute. In all there are more than 200 ancient *ahuehuetes* growing in Azcapotzalco. Throughout the Valley of Mexico, other *ahuehuetes* stand as witnesses to the pre-Hispanic past, including one named 'El Sargento' in Chapultepec, and one under which Cortés cried after his forces were expelled from Tenochtitlan on what is now known in Mexico (in Spanish) as the *Noche Victoriosa* (Victorious Night).

Another reminder of Aztec ingenuity, alluded to above, is to be found in Xochimilco, one of the original regions of chinampa culture, where the platforms that so impressed Díaz del Castillo still flourish (Figure 6). There is a lingering misapprehension that a chinampa can be described as a floating garden. According to Zelia Nuttall, in his eighteenth century *Historia Antigua de México*, the Mexican historian Francisco Clavijero frequently referred to chinampas as 'floating gardens' - as they sometimes still are. In Nuttall's view Clavijero had misinterpreted sixteenth-century indigenous scholar Alvarado de Tezozómoc's explanations of how chinampas were constructed. Instead she argued that 'floating gardens' were the result of the innovations of the seed starters and the rafts needed to transport the tribute demanded by the Azcapotzalcans discussed above.[22] More recent scholars concur. For example, in an article entitled 'Gardens in Swamps', Pedro Armillas confirms that the legend of the floating gardens of Moctezuma's reign and the theory that the contemporary 'land-based' chinampas were relics of these original floating gardens appear 'to have arisen through errors of observation made by some witnesses who mistook the movable nurseries for the farm plots.'[23]

The loss of chinampa culture due to the rapid urbanization which took place in Mexico in the last decades of the nineteenth century and early years of the twentieth was something that Zelia Nuttall also had cause to lament.[24] Although the process has continued since then, she might have been heartened by the news that in recent years the Mexican government has been funding the expansion of chinampa culture in Xochimilco with a view to regenerating some of the 5,000 acres of chinampas. An article by Alejandra Borunda in *National Geographic* explains that:

> The COVID-19 pandemic gave chinampa proponents an unexpected boost: when food supply chain disruptions and lockdowns shut down produce flows to the city, chinamperos connected directly with customers, boosting their profile and sales—and reminding consumers that there is a long, storied agricultural legacy within their own city limits.[25]

By the time of the pandemic, the United Nations Food and Agriculture Organization (FAO) had already, in 2018, included Mexico's chinampa culture in its list of fifty landscape environments designated as Important Global Agricultural Heritage Systems, citing how it:

> 'stands out for having a great biodiversity: It houses 2% of the world's biodiversity and 11% of the national biodiversity with 139 species of vertebrates, 21 species of fish, six amphibians, 10 species of reptiles, 79 species of birds and 23 species of mammals.
> It also stands out for preserving ancestral agricultural knowledge and technologies, as chinamperos farmers preserve traditional prehispanic cultivation techniques that have been transmitted orally: in the chinampas you can still find four of the five main crops used by the Aztecs: corn, beans, pumpkin, and amaranth.'[26]

Figure 6: Aerial view of chinampa platforms from present-day Xochimilco.
Photo: courtesy of UN Food and Agriculture Organization.

CONCLUSION

The Aztecs constructed their spectacular garden palaces as both retreats and demonstrations of their dominion over vassal cities, the source not just of their wealth but also of the exotic plants which enhanced the show of power. That power, however, could not have been achieved without developing the intensive agricultural methods of chinampa farming, a technique that is seeing a renaissance today.

REFERENCES

[1] Nahuatl was the language of the Aztecs and is still used today by about 1.5 million people in central Mexico. Unless otherwise stated, all the foreign-language terms used in this paper are Nahuatl.

[2] Pascual de Gayangos (ed), *Cartas y relaciones de Hernan Cortés al Emperador Carlos V*, (Paris: Emprenta Central de los Ferro-Carriles, 1866), p.83, quotation translated by author.

[3] Bernal Díaz del Castillo, *Historia verdadera de la conquista de la Nueva España*, 1621 (Mexico City: Editorial Pedro Robredo, 1939), p. 308, quotation translated by author.

[4] Díaz del Castillo, p. 309.

[5] Gayangos, p. 83.

[6] Richard Blanton, 'Prehispanic Adaptation in the Ixtapalapa Region, Mexico.' *Science*, 24 March 2011, pp. 1317-26 (p.1320).

[7] Díaz del Castillo, p. 302.

[8] The Aztec Triple Alliance was one forged between the city -states of Tenochtitlan, Tlacopan and Texcoco, often referred to as the Aztec Empire. See, for example, David Roos, 'How the Aztec Empire was Forged Through a Triple Alliance', *History*, 24 February 2021.

[9] Robert C. West and Pedro Armillas, 'Las chinampas de México: poesía y realidad de los jardines flotantes,' *Cuadernos Americanos,* 50 (Mexico, 1950), p. 168.

[10] Zelia Nuttall, *Los Jardines Del Antiguo Mexico* (Mexico: Sociedad Scientífica Antonio Alzate, 1920), p. 209.

[11] Nuttall, pp. 207-8.

[12] Nuttall, quoting from Juan de Tovar's *Codice Ramirez*. *Relación del origen de los indios que habitan esta Nueva España,* 1587, pp. 210-11.

[13] Nuttall, p. 211.

[14] Nuttall, p. 211

[15] Nuttall, p. 209.

[16] Katherine Ashenberg, 'Clean Aztecs, Dirty Spaniards', *Aztecs at Mexicolore,* *www.mexicolore.co.uk/aztecs/home/clean-aztecs-dirty-spaniards* [accessed 29 January 2023]

[17] Michael Smith, 'Life in the Provinces of the Aztec Empire', *Scientific American* 2005. Archived (PDF) from the original on 21 January 2021. https://web.archive.org/web/20210121101721/http://www.public.asu.edu/~mesmith9/MES-05-SciAm-.pdf, [accessed 10 February 2023].

[18] Jeanne Gillespie and Nicolle Jordan, 'Aztec Gardens: Representations of Political Power, Innovation, and Technology', *The Southern Quarterly,* 57.1 (2019), pp. 23-43 (pp. 38-42); Patricia Granziera, 'Concept of the Garden in Pre-Hispanic Mexico', *Garden History*, 29:2 (2001), pp. 185-213 (p.185).

[19] Gillespie and Jordan, pp. 38-42; Granziera, p. 190. On this page Granziera lists some of the plants brought to Huastepec.

[20] Díaz del Castillo, p.309

[21] Nuttall, p. 207

[22] Nuttall, p. 207

[23] Pedro Armillas, 'Gardens on Swamps, *Science,* 12 November 1971, pp. 653-61 (p.653)

[24] Nuttall, p.207. On the urbanization of Mexico see, for example, Robert V. Kemper and Anya Peterson Royce, 'Mexican Urbanization Since 1821: A Macro-Historical Approach, *Urban Anthropology,* 8:3/4 (1979), pp. 267-89.

[25] Alejandra Borunda, 'In Mexico City, the pandemic revived Aztec-era island farms', *National Geographic Environment*, June 22 2022, https://www.nationalgeographic.com/magazine/article/in-mexico-city-the-pandemic-revived-aztec-era-island-farms [accessed 12 February 2023].

[26] United Nations Food and Agriculture Organization 'Chinampas of Mexico City were recognized as an Agricultural Heritage System of Global Importance' https://www.fao.org/americas/noticias/ver/en/c/1118851/ [accessed 10 February 2023].

ARANJUEZ: MIRROR OF THE POLITICAL IDEA OF THE BURGUNDIAN GARDEN

MARGARET GOEHRING

ABSTRACT

This paper argues that when King Philip II of Spain (1527-1598) developed the landscape of his palace at Aranjuez, the Burgundian gardens of the Low Countries and Northern France were highly influential. The Burgundian influence is found not only in aspects of the layout, engineering and plantings at Aranjuez, but also in the way that the gardens function in promoting the king's conceptions of noble identity and rulership. Indeed, Aranjuez represents a culmination of the long history of the 'Burgundian Garden' as a political symbol and tool of state formation.

INTRODUCTION

As any gardener knows, the garden is always in a state of becoming. As such, it is as much an idea as it is a physical space; within the garden we are also interacting with the idea of the garden. The garden both frames and is an agent in producing particular behaviours. What we do in a garden is often ritualistic, from the methodical routines of caring for the garden, which is subject to a regular seasonal order, to the ways in which we move through a garden, led by paths or stopping to admire carefully managed features. In effect, the garden sets a 'horizon of expectation'[1] as much as any work of literature or art does. The rulers of the Burgundian Valois-Habsburg dynasty of the late Middle Ages and Renaissance were particularly aware of the potential of the garden to activate meaning, and they exploited their gardens as a powerful tool of early state formation, using them to frame and elicit noble identity and rulership.[2]

The Valois-Burgundian rulers of Northern France and the Low Countries developed a distinctive garden idea, which I have called the 'Burgundian garden'.[3] The Burgundian garden is not defined so much by any specific or distinctive formal characteristics, nor can it be neatly categorized as being 'Medieval' or 'Renaissance'. It is an idea comprised of both physical and symbolic gardens, actual spaces and emblems. While rooted in the French royal gardens of the fourteenth century, the Burgundian garden became a distinct idea by the end of the fifteenth century, and was closely tied to Valois-Burgundian performances of magnificence and nobility. In the sixteenth century, Burgundian-Habsburg rulers would magnify this concept on a massive scale that would continue to inform gardens well into the seventeenth and eighteenth centuries. Nowhere is this as apparent as at the royal palace of Aranjuez.

THE GARDENS OF ARANJUEZ

Located at the confluence of the Tajo and Jarama rivers, Aranjuez was one of a string of palaces surrounding Madrid that King Philip II developed as a way to enhance the city's status as Spain's new capital.[4] Aranjuez was one of the largest and most ambitious of these estates, and Philip II began working on its landscape in the 1550s, well before he began work on the palace itself. His ambition was ultimately to connect Aranjuez to the Atlantic by making the Tajo River navigable along its entire length.

Although this was never achieved, Philip II intended at one point for the estate to be a focal point of his rulership. As Albert Postma has characterized it:

> The total concept of the garden and landscape architecture at Aranjuez implied far-reaching symbolism. Neither allegorical images nor iconographic programs gave expression to the ideas of Philip II, rather, the domain as a whole was the carrier of a conceptual program meant to represent the harmony and coherence of his [own] Garden of Eden. Aranjuez was the artificial universe of Philip II encompassing both nature and art, as well as court life.[5]

Aranjuez introduced a new type of country estate to Spain. Rather than using their country houses as temporary domiciles, as was common in France, Italy and Flanders, the Spanish nobility had traditionally tended to take only short excursions in order to enjoy the mixture of cultivated lands and rustic wilderness. Therefore their estates were not significantly developed to the same extent as their northern counterparts.[6] However, Aranjuez offered considerably expanded amenities, including a hunting park stocked with fallow deer, wild boar, hares, rabbits and wolves; ornamental orchards; flowering herb-filled meadows and various types of gardens; paved, tree-lined paths and allées; brick-lined canals, dams and sluices; ponds stocked with swans and carp imported from France; agricultural crops including almonds, wheat and barley as well as ornamental and exotic flowers; a cattle and horse breeding programme; and a distillery. The centrepiece was an artificial island at the junction of the two rivers known as La Isla, which had its own gardens of jasmine, tulips, amaryllis, boxwood, fruit trees, grapes and vegetables.

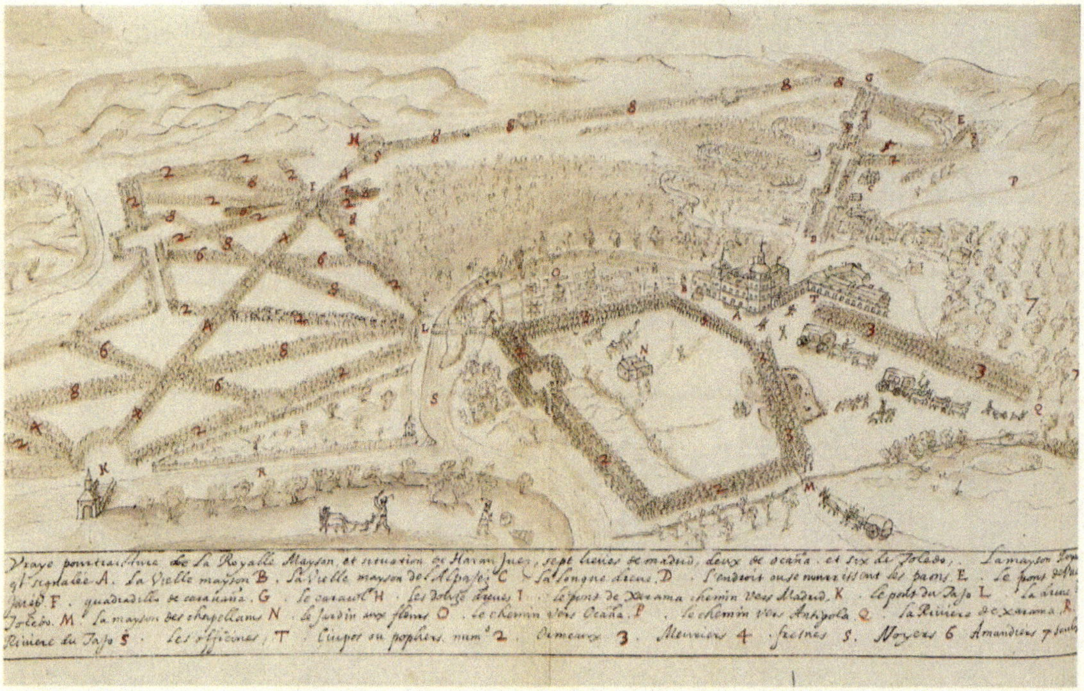

Figure 1. Jehan l'Hermite, *Plan of Aranjuez* from *Le passe-temps: Mémoire d'un gentilhomme de la Chambre de Philippe II, de 1587 à 1602* (Brussels KBR MS. II 1028)

As with many elite gardens of the sixteenth century, Aranjuez reflected Italian influences. Its principal architect was the Italian-educated Juan Bautista de Toledo after whose death in 1567 Philip II appointed Juan de Herrera, a mathematician and architect, to continue the design.[7] The geometric arrangement of plantings and symmetrical organization of some of the gardens, especially the parterre gardens, showcased Italian design influences. Many of these and other elements are seen on a plan, looking northward, drawn by Jehan l'Hermite (Figure 1).

Aranjuez also included uncultivated wooded areas on the bank of the Tajo River, which were separate from the hunting park and which provided a backdrop when viewed from the main gardens to the west of the palace. These woods were described by Luis Gómez de Tapia in 1582:

en la interior ribera está plantado
un bosquet tal, que desde allí su fuente
ni hasta el Oceano lusitano,
no se halla en otra parte más ufano.
Tiene árboles de especie diferentes,
parte plantados, parte allí nascidos,
parte en el cristalino río pendientes,
y parte por el llano repartidos...[8]

[...on the interior bank is planted
a forest, from its source
not even to the Lusitanian Ocean,
one could not find it in a prouder place.
It has trees of different species,
partly planted, partly there born,
partly bending over the crystalline river,
and partly distributed over the plain.]

The encomium goes on to state that these woods are the home of naiads, sprites and dryads, along with other pastoral mythological beings, recalling the Italian concept of the *bosco*.[9] However, unlike many Italian boscos, which were designed with pathways and seating to induce visitors to spend time within them, the woods at Aranjuez did not include such comforts.[10] The inspiration for this woodland seems to have had a different source. It is possible the woodlands may have been inspired by the Spanish appreciation of contrasts in rustic and cultivated landscapes, as mentioned earlier; however, the scale of the area seems to have been influenced by a more Northern European appreciation of the forest as a site of fecundity. While Medieval literature often presented the forest as a desolate, terrifying wilderness, by the late Middle Ages forests were highly prized assets, associated more with adventure, love and spiritual vision.[11] Primarily esteemed as hunting sites, forests were also valued for their natural resources and for their aesthetic qualities—especially forests contained within elite estates. This can be seen, for example, in the avenues that crossed through the forest at the famed park at Hesdin (Pas-de-Calais), which to this day still maintain their late Medieval names—'li vert chemin' and 'li chemin de Fontaine aux Dames'—highlighting beautiful aspects of the site.[12] Images of forests were also found on tapestries and murals as seen, for example, in the fourteenth-century murals of forest scenery populated by playing children that were painted in the queen's apartments at the Hôtel de Saint-Pol.[13] Clearly referencing the trope of fecundity, the association of the forest with rich fruitfulness is also apparent in fifteenth-century French and Flemish books of hours wherein the month of May was illustrated with aristocratic men and women going into the forests to collect greenery as part of the spring celebrations. One particular example can be found in the *Très Riches Heures* of Jean de Berry from before 1416.[14] An appreciation of the fertility and fecundity of the forest was such that by the sixteenth century paradise itself, the Garden of Eden, was visualized as a dense yet bountiful wood rather than as an enclosed garden.[15] At Aranjuez, the semi-cultivated woods would have provided a lushly verdant backdrop to the rich abundance of the formal gardens, fostering the perception of the site as a paradise. Indeed, Gómez de Tapia made this precise association, linking paradise, fecundity and the woods of Aranjuez throughout his encomium.[16]

NORTHERN EUROPEAN INFLUENCES ON ARANJUEZ

Aranjuez was in other ways more reflective of the great princely estates of Northern Europe, especially those of the Burgundian Valois-Hapsburg dynasty, than of the traditions of either Italy or Spain. Philip II so admired the expertise of Flemish gardeners and engineers that he imported several from the Low Countries, many of whom had worked for his aunt, Mary of Hungary.[17] Chief among them was Jehan Holbecq who was at Aranjuez by the end of January 1561 and who worked with the Spanish head-gardener, Jerónimo de Algora, in creating the Isla garden. Originally designed by Bautista de Toledo, La Isla was considerably altered by Holbecq on the basis of his Netherlandish experience. Over time, Holbecq's aesthetic could be seen in the rest of the gardens, with the addition of northern elements such as *allées* lined with fruiting and/or pleached trees, high hawthorn hedgerows, shaded walkways, trellises and even a labyrinth. Holbecq also brought in Netherlandish gardening tools and equipment, and introduced numerous flowers, trees, herbs and vegetables from Flanders.[18]

On Holbecq's recommendation, Philip II had thousands of trees—particularly poplars—imported from Flanders to line the paths and canals across the estate, and especially in a part of the estate known as the 'Pico Tajo', seen on the left side of l'Hermite's drawing. The Pico Tajo consisted of tree-lined radiating avenues that separated various agricultural fields and orchards into triangular units. The complex symbolism of this design was informed by nautical charts and new mathematical ideas rooted in Platonic theory that linked Aranjuez to universal cosmography and contemporary cartography.[19] Unlike the other paths and roads on the estate which provided access to the palace or other points, the paths of the Pico Tajo were created solely for the purpose of walking and riding and did not go to any particular destinations. These avenues also seem to have been used as stages for festive combats and other entertainments such as bullfights and dances.[20] At the same time, from the ground, the aspect of tree-lined canals and avenues dividing agricultural fields would have given a distinctively Netherlandish character to the Aranjuez landscape.

Philip II had been introduced to the Netherlandish landscape in 1548-1549 during a grand tour of Europe organized by his father, Charles V, Holy Roman Emperor (r. 1519-1556), to introduce the young prince to his future subjects and establish his legitimacy as heir to the realm. Elite Burgundian gardens, especially the Coudenberg, Binche and Mariemont (see below), played starring roles in this tour, reflecting a long-standing practice of using princely gardens to symbolize rulership and political unity within the Burgundian Valois-Habsburg lineage.

THE BURGUNDIAN GARDEN

As I have articulated elsewhere, the concept of the 'Burgundian Garden' is rooted in the gardens of the first Valois kings who particularly developed the garden as a site of royal identity and magnificence.[21] In the early-fourteenth century, the 'Jardin du palaiz du roy' at the Palais de la Cité in Paris was a site of Capetian political authority and used as a staging ground for duels and punishments.[22] King Philip VI (1293-1350) later augmented the luxurious amenities of the Palais de la Cité, adding a private boat dock on the Seine, and a three-storey house at the bottom of the garden in which the future Charles V of France (r.1364-1380) resided when visiting the palace. Philip VI also installed private gardens to support the health of his future dynasty. At his orders, a pleasure garden with trellises, flowering meadows, and wooden pavilions covered by vines was planted at the Abbey of Maubisson in 1335 for one of the pregnancies of Jeanne de Bourgogne. He ordered this garden to be replicated a few months later ('aussi comme l'en avoit fait en l'abbaie de Maubuisson') at the royal residence at the Palais de la Cité for the benefit of his son (who was convalescing from illness) and pregnant daughter-in-law.[23]

Charles V amplified the use of the garden to promote his identity in a way that was both public and private at the same time. For example, while the gardens at his favoured residence, the Hôtel de Saint-Pol, were enclosed by high walls, the accounts indicate that these were ornamented with the Valois emblem, the fleur-de-lys. As Christine de Pizan noted in her biography of the king, he would spend time every day in his gardens meeting with family, and favoured merchants and ambassadors who were admitted via a special entrance of their own.[24] The writer connected this routine to his ordered life, as well as to his health and to the health of his governance.[25]

Charles V would have known one of the most spectacular and famous gardens of the Middle Ages: Hesdin.[26] Established by Robert II, Count of Artois in 1288, it came into the possession of the Valois Burgundian dukes by the third quarter of the fourteenth century. It was the site of royal weddings, and the highest echelons of society often visited it (Figure 2). The estate included a forest whose trees were carefully maintained to protect mounted hunters from branches; a menagerie and heronry; flowering meadows; springs and fountains; fruiting trees and herbs; and rose bowers. It also contained fabulous automata inspired by literary romance, including a bridge with badger-fur covered monkeys that waved; a statue of a hermit that spoke; a golden tree with singing mechanical birds; and a gallery with murals depicting the story of Jason and the Golden Fleece that were accompanied by special effects, including thunder, lightning and rain. Under Duke Philip the Good of Burgundy (1396-1467), in the fifteenth century Hesdin achieved near mythical fame. Used for important political events, treaty negotiations and elaborately staged receptions, Hesdin became part of the apparatus of Burgundian displays of magnificence that were crucial to manifesting the duke's authority and framing his political ambitions to become a prince in his own right.[27]

The idea of using the garden as a site for proclaiming personal identity and political authority had been exploited even earlier by the duke's grandparents, Philip the Bold of Burgundy (1342-1404) and Margaret of Flanders (d. 1405). At the Château de Germolles, for example, Margaret spent over 19,000 francs between 1381 and 1393 upgrading the amenities and magnificence of the estate.[28] The ornamentation was largely designed to portray the ducal couple as Good Shepherds. Besides commissioning multiple murals and tapestries with sheep and shepherding imagery, Margaret also had

Figure 2. Fête Champetre à la Cour de Bourgogne, seventeenth-century copy after a work of c. 1420 (Dijon: © Musée des Beaux-Arts)

her saddles embroidered with gilt copper sheep, the headboards of the beds quilted with sheep in silk and gold, and jewellery made featuring sheep and garden imagery. The centrepiece was a sculpted portrait by Claus Sluter of the duke and duchess standing in a garden under a gilded tree surrounded by sheep.[29]

THE GARDEN AS POLITICAL EMBLEM

The garden ultimately became entrenched as an emblem of the Valois line, due in part to its analogy with the fleur-de-lys, the Valois monarchical symbol. This idea was also closely related to the concept of the 'Garden of France', exemplified in a late fifteenth-century frontispiece for Guillaume de Nangis' historical chronicle of the kings of France—known as the *Chronique Abrégée*– showing the kings in an enclosed garden with the fleur-de-lys device and armorials (Figure 3).

This trope would routinely appear in political propaganda and performances over the course of the following century. Temporary symbolic gardens were often used as part of Triumphal Entries, presenting the city as a paradise unified in peaceful harmony under the entering ruler. At the Entries of Charles VIII of France into Paris in 1484 and 1492 the Fontaine du Ponceau was made to emit wine

Figure 3. Detail from Anon, Frontispiece for Guillaume de Nangis, *Chronique Abrégée*, manuscript illumination, c.1470 (Bibliothèque nationale de France MS. Fr. 2598, fol. 1r).

and was surrounded by a symbolic garden representing the 'clos de Paris'. At Anne of Brittany's Entry into Paris in 1504 the royal court of justice, known as the Châtelet, was transformed into a garden populated by shepherds and shepherdesses singing hymns of peace and unity.[30] This same theme was repeated for the Entry of Mary Tudor and Louis XII in Paris in 1514 as recorded in a festival book commemorating the event.[31]

The 1433 Seal of Jacqueline of Bavaria (d. 1436) offers an interesting variation of the garden as an emblem of political identity and unity (Figure 4). The granddaughter of Duke Philip the Bold, and as her father's only legitimate offspring, Jacqueline inherited the counties of Holland, Zeeland and Hainaut. However, her cousin, Philip the Good also sought control of these wealthy lands. The wars that resulted devastated the region, and Jacqueline had been forced into giving up her regency and titles by the time she had the seal made. The seal shows the coats of arms of the counties within an enclosed garden, over which appear the Virgin and Child. Besides the obvious religious symbolism linking female rulership with the Virgin Mary and the *hortus conclusus*, the heraldic lions bearing the Bavarian-Hainaut armorials suggest a more overt political message about the Garden of Hainaut, Holland and Zeeland as a site of peace and unity.[32]

In parallel with the 'Garden of France' and the 'Garden of Hainaut', emblematic invocations of the 'Garden of Burgundy' appeared in court festivities and in political propaganda. At the marriage of Philip the Good to Isabella of Portugal in 1430, the central hall of the ducal palace was transformed into a garden dominated by a golden tree from which hung the armorials of all the Burgundian nobility.[33] This motif was later recreated at the marriage of Charles the Bold and Margaret of York in 1468. In turn Emperor Maximilian of Austria (1459-1519) would adopt the iconography of the 'Garden of Burgundy' to stress his unity with his Burgundian/Netherlandish subjects, especially after the death of his wife, Mary of Burgundy, in 1482.

Figure 4. Seal of Jacqueline of Bavaria, 1432 (Valenciennes: Archives Municipales 8 JJ 3-1) Wikimedia Commons

Beginning around 1505, the emperor collaborated with his secretary, Marx Treitzsauerwein, in writing his pseudo-autobiography, *Der Weisskunig* (The White King), which was written as a chivalric romance. Although never completed, a partial version was published in 1526. For the narrative recounting his marriage to Mary of Burgundy, the accompanying woodcut shows Maximilian becoming acculturated to Burgundian magnificence within a beautiful garden as the pair learn each other's languages.[34] In 1515, he commissioned a choir-book for Charles, the opening miniature of which shows the future emperor in an enclosed garden.[35] Accompanied by his siblings, the representatives of the three estates and the imperial arms, this miniature emphasized the image of Charles V as a divinely ordained ruler within the *hortus conclusus* of the Burgundian Netherlands.[36] The garden of unity was also enacted that same year in a tableau on the occasion of Charles' entry into Bruges, in which Charles was presented as Orpheus unifying his vast territories in a paradisal garden.[37]

THE BURGUNDIAN GARDEN AND THE HAPSBURGS: THE COUDENBERG

By this point the foremost Burgundian garden was at the Coudenberg Palace in Brussels.[38] Originally the palace of the Dukes of Brabant, Philip the Good acquired it in 1434. He expanded its enclosed hunting park, known as the 'Warrande', and added a ball court and a tournament field. The estate also included a pleasure garden, with 1,000 fruiting trees, a large pond known as the 'Cloutinc' next to an enclosed parterre garden, and a larger enclosed garden known as the 'Labyrinthe' that included a four-storey wooden pavilion for the private use of the duke and his family. In the early sixteenth century the Coudenberg was the favoured residence of Duke Philip the Fair (d. 1506) and his wife, Joanna of Castile (d. 1555). Its centrality to their rulership is seen in the wing panels of a triptych that was commissioned for the judicial chambers of the 'Vierschaar' in Zeeland before 1506, where Philip and Joanna are shown in full armorials standing within the 'Warrande' of the Coudenberg.[39]

Under Emperor Charles V and his sister, Mary of Hungary (1505-1558), whom he appointed regent of the Netherlands, the Coudenberg continued to symbolize Habsburg dominion. The pair further enlarged the Warrande and augmented the menagerie into a veritable zoological *Wunderkammer* with ostriches, camels, turkeys, leopards and other exotic animals. The 'Labyrinthe'—now called the 'Feuillée'—was planted with laurel and rosemary topiaries and hawthorn arbours, and new fountains with classical subjects were installed. The centrepiece was a new marble-columned pavilion decorated with Habsburg armorials, lions, golden apples and statues of saints and heroes.

Representations of the Coudenberg as seen from the Warrande significantly outnumber the city-side view of the palace with its ceremonial courtyard, suggesting that the gardens and park were by far the more important symbols of Habsburg rulership. One of the most enduring and replicated views of the Coudenberg first appears in a painting from around 1540 attributed to Lucas van Gassel, which in turn was based on a much earlier study (Figure 5).[40] The neighbouring Hôtel Hoogstraten and Hôtel Nassau are shown in both their states before 1520, while the monumental classical gallery constructed between 1533 and 1537, which housed Mary of Hungary's private apartments, reception spaces and art collection, dominates the view at the left. To the right, only the two lower storeys of the great chapel (begun in 1522) are seen; the third storey was not constructed until the early 1550s. The foreground of the painting shows the ballcourt, jousting field, the Cloutinc pond and the Feuillée (Labyrinthe). This same view appears in a second version that shows the palace at the same state as it appeared around 1540, but now updated with seventeenth-century style parterre gardens.[41] Curiously, this outdated view would continue to be copied well into the second half of the seventeenth century in prints and maps.[42]

Figure 5. Lucas Gassel (attr.), *View of the Coudenberg*, c. 1540 (Brussels: City Museum MVB K-1941-1) Wikimedia Commons

The Warrande is also seen in a tapestry from a celebrated series of the *Chasses de Maximilien*, designed around 1531 by Bernard van Orley. While the original tapestry series no longer survives, its popularity and significance are attested to by the fact that two copies from the seventeenth century are extant.[43] The series depicts the twelve months of the year, each one representing Maximilian hunting at different imperial sites in and around Brussels. The month of March shows Maximilian on horseback in the Warrande looking back to the palace and its gardens. Perhaps commissioned by Mary of Hungary, the series seems to have been intended to symbolize the unity of Habsburg rulership between the emperor and his regents through this imperial ritual.[44]

MARY OF HUNGARY AND THE BURGUNDIAN GARDEN: BINCHE AND MARIEMONT

Mary of Hungary was instrumental in fostering the development of the Burgundian garden at her other estates, especially at Binche and Mariemont, both of which were significant influences on Aranjuez. Mariemont was a hunting lodge that functioned as a satellite estate to Binche. Set within 483 hectares, Mariemont was designed and built between 1546 and 1549 by favoured architect, Jacques du Broeucq.[45] Emulating Chambord, albeit on a smaller scale, Mariemont was built on top of a raised platform, surrounded by a paved moat and set within a pattern of gardens, ponds, and orchards that were oriented along the axes of the palace itself (Figure 6).[46]

The estate also included farms, vineyards, livestock and woodland. The gardens were created by Jehan Holbecq (whom Philip II would later bring to Spain) in 1546-1547, working with a team of Flemish gardeners. One of the gardens was clearly inspired by the Feuillée at the Coudenberg, including similar green fencing and a wooden arbour supporting hawthorns. Another garden, called the 'jardin à jolietez', was planted with flowers and a vast variety of imported fruits and rosemary topiaries and enclosed with blackberry and hawthorn hedges. A more formal, ceremonial garden consisted of a series

Figure 6. Jan Brueghel the Elder, *View of Mariemont*, 1612 (Dijon: © Musée des Beaux-Arts / photo François Jay)

of large terraces planted with rare flowers and vegetables and divided into quadrants by brick-paved paths and dominated by a large, central fountain designed by Du Broeucq.[47] There were also wooded areas, one of which bordering the formal gardens was planted with trees in neat rows, while other areas were kept more natural to provide pleasingly verdant backdrops. As a visitor to the estate in 1549 described the effect:

> *....ce ne sont partout que frais ombrages, parterres fleuris, fontaines limpides, entourés d'une ceinture d'etangs et de beaux et grands bois qui encadrent une perspective etendue de plaines verdoyantes et de bosquets odoriferants, ou l'on voit bondir des troupeaux de cerfs....*[48]
>
> [...Everywhere there is nothing but cool shade, flowerbeds, limpid fountains, surrounded by a belt of ponds and beautiful and large woods which frame an extended perspective of verdant plains and fragrant groves, where one sees leaping herds of deer...].

The most famous and celebrated of Mary's estates was Binche. Originally owned by the counts of Hainaut, Charles V presented Binche to his sister in 1545. She then built a magnificent palace within its Medieval walls, with the intention of rivalling Fontainebleau. On the south side of the palace, protected from the winter winds by the walls of the chapel, was an enclosed 'petit Jardin' (also called a 'jardin a jolietez emprès la grant salle') that accommodated a wood-framed orangery, and beds planted with exotic flowers, including Spanish violets, marjoram and roses — all in the colours of the royal arms of Spain and Hungary.[49] To the north of the central courtyard was a parterre 'grand jardin' that was dominated by an elegant fountain of Rance marble. Here the parterres were planted with vines, apricot trees, potted flowers and herbs. This garden was also adorned with statues of ancient heroes displayed in niches, of which a figure of Cleopatra and the Nile survive. Finally, there was an enclosed 'jardin nouveau' also with a northern exposure that had panoramic views to the east and alder -wood covered paths for summer walking.

These massive projects were completed just in time for the extended tour of the imperial realms that the emperor organized for his son, Philip II, in 1548-1549. The culmination of the tour were games held at Binche and Mariemont designed to integrate the Castilian-born Philip into Burgundian chivalric culture and underscore his dynastic validity.[50] The development of Binche and Mariemont as vital images of Habsburg unity and imperial power did not stop with the future Philip II's visit. Mary continued to embellish the gardens, including commissioning copies of the casts of famous ancient statues that Primaticcio had made for Fontainebleau, as well as six life-size bronze portraits, of which only those of the emperor and Mary herself survive. She also had an ephemeral triumphal arch from the 1549 games, which was modelled on the Arch of Constantine, restored and reassembled in the 'jardin nouveau' at Binche in 1553. The entire design of the gardens and their ornamentation seem to have been part of a coherent programme to eulogize Charles V's imperial ambitions.[51]

THE LEGACY AT ARANJUEZ

The political significance of Binche and Mariemont was not lost on others. Indeed, both were attacked in 1554 by the armies of Henry II who was intent on wresting power from the Emperor and Mary of

Hungary. While Mariemont was restored and continued to be a favoured residence under Archdukes Albert and Isabella (r. 1598-1633,) Binche was largely destroyed and abandoned by the end of the century.

However, Binche, like the other Burgundian estates, had left an indelible impression on the heir to the Spanish throne. Once installed as king in 1556, Philip determined to make Madrid the undisputed centre of his realm, a strategy that involved the development of royal properties around the capital. The gardens attached to these estates combined influences from the Low Countries, Italy and France in a novel way: at the same time, though, they were very much rooted within a long-standing tradition of conceiving the garden as a political site, an idea encapsulated in the concept of the Burgundian garden.

REFERENCES

[1] Hans Robert Jauss, *Toward an Aesthetic of Reception*, trans. by Timothy Bahti (Minneapolis: University of Minnesota Press, 1982), Chapter 1

[2] For an excellent overview of the Burgundian Valois dynasty, see Richard Vaughan, *The Dukes of Burgundy*, by Richard Vaughan (Rochester/Suffolk: Boydell Press, 2002), as well as Wim Blockmans and Walter Prevenier, *The Low Countries Under Burgundian Rule, 1369-1530,* trans. by Elizabeth Fackelman, (Philadelphia: University of Pennsylvania Press, 1988).

[3] Margaret Goehring, 'The Politics of Space of the Burgundian Garden', in *Landscape and the Visual Hermeneutics of Place, 1500-1700*, ed. by Walter Melion & Karl Enenkel (Leiden: Brill, 2020), pp. 326-66.

[4] Albert Postma, 'Een Zuidnederlandse hovenier in Spanje: Over Filips II, Jehan Holbecq en een nieuwe tuinkuns', *Tuinkuns: Nederlands Jaarboek voor de Geschiedenis van Tuin- en Landschapsarchitectuur* 1 (1995), pp. 9-22 (p. 10).

[5] Postma (1995), p. 11; all translations in this paper have been done by me, including any errors, unless otherwise noted.

[6] Catherine Wilkinson Zermer, 'European Convergences: Philippe II and the Landscape of Aranjuez', in *Architecture, Jardin, Paysage: L'Environnement du château et de la villa aux XVe et XVIe Siècles (Actes du colloque tenu à Tours du 1er au 4 juin 1992)*, ed by Jean Guillaume, (Tours/Picard, 1999), pp. 243-58.

[7] For a thorough discussion of the genesis and history of the landscape, see Ana Luengo Añón, *Aranjuez, Utopia y Realidad: La Construcción de un Paisaje* (Madrid: Instituto de Estudios Madrileños, 2008).

[8] Gómez de Tapia, 'Egloga pastoril en que se describe el bosque de Aranjuez y el nascimiento de la serenísima infanta doña Isabel de España', in *Libro de la Montería* (Seville: Andrea Pescini, 1582), lines 1049-1056; the forest of the hunting park is described earlier at lines 152-159.

[9] Gómez de Tapia (1582), ll. 219-27.

[10] See Claudia Lazzaro, *The Italian Renaissance Garden: From the Conventions of Planting, Design, and Ornament to the Grand Gardens of Sixteenth-Century Central Italy* (New Haven: Yale University Press, 1990), Chapter 5.

[11] Albrecht Classen, *The Forest in Medieval German Literature: Ecocritical Readings from a Historical Perspective*, (Maryland: Lexington Books, 2015); Corrine J. Saunders, *The Forest of Medieval Romance: Avernus, Broceliande, Arden* (Cambridge: D.S. Brewer, 1993).

[12] Sharon Farmer, 'Aristocratic Power and the "Natural" Landscape: The Garden Park at Hesdin, ca. 1291-1302', *Speculum* 88 (2013), pp. 644-80.

[13] Christian de Mérindol, 'Essai sur la distinction des espaces par le décor à l'époque médiévale: iconologie et topographie', in *'Aux marches du Palais'. Qu'est-ce qu'un palais médiéval ? Données historiques et archéologiques*. Actes du VIIe Congrès international d'Archéologie Médiévale, Le Mans – Mayenne 9-11 septembre 1999, (Caen : Société d'Archéologie Médiévale, 2001), pp. 63-75.

[14] For example, *Très Riches Heures* of Duke Jean de Berry (Chantilly, Musée Condé).

[15] For example, Albrecht Dürer, *Adam and Eve*, engraving, 1504 (Metropolitan Museum of Art 19.73.1); Jan Sadeler (after Maarten de Vos), *The Sixth Day: The Creation of Adam, Eve and the Animals*, engraving, around 1587 (Philadelphia Museum of Art 1961-85-675).

[16] Gómez de Tapia (1582), ll. 13-22, 25-32, 152-159, 285-291.
[17] For full list, see Postma, p. 12.
[18] Postma, p. 17.
[19] Ana Luengo, 'El Real Sitio de Aranjuez', in *Parámetros del Jardín Español [Naturaleza-Paisaje-Territorio]*, ed. by Ana Luengo and Coro Milleres, 3 vols (Madrid: Ministerio de Cultura, 2007), II: pp. 54-65 (pp. 57-60), and idem, 2nd edn (2008), especially Chapter 2.
[20] Zermer, p. 246 and fn. 22; this function is also alluded to in Gómez de Tapia's eulogy, (ll. 227-31) as the site where naiads, dryads and other pastoral deities danced.
[21] Goehring (2020).
[22] A. Hellot (ed), 'Chronique parisienne anonyme de 1316 a 1339', *Memoires de la Société de l'Histoire de Paris*, XI (1885), pp. 31-32, 39, 54 and 108 (No.s 16, 28, 55, 56, 155)
[23] Hellot, (1885), pp. 163-64 (No.s 264, 265).
[24] Christine de Pizan, *Le Livre des faits et bonnes moeurs du roi Charles V le Sage*, trans. by Eric Hicks and Thérèse Moreau, (Paris: Stock/Moyen Age, 1997), Part I, pp.16, 67-70.
[25] Goehring (2020), pp. 334-35; this idea is also reflected in Piero de Crescenzi's *Liber ruralium*, which was translated into French at the orders of the king in 1371; see J. Bauman, 'Tradition and Transformation: The Pleasure Garden in Piero de' Crescenzi's *Liber ruralium commodorium*', *Studies in the History of Gardens & Designed Landscapes,* 22:2 (2002), pp. 99-141 (p. 103).
[26] For review of the principal literature on Hesdin, see Margaret Goehring, 'Artifice and Ornament in the *Dit dou Lyon* Garden Miniature', in *Poetry, Art, and Music in Guillaume de Machaut's Earliest Manuscript (BnF fr. 1586)*, ed. by Lawrence Earp & Jared Hartt (Turnhout: Brepols, 2021), pp. 217-37.
[27] Goehring (2020), pp. 328-30. On Philip the Good's political ambitions, see C.A.J. Armstrong, *England, France, and Burgundy in the Fifteenth Century* (London: Hambledon Press, 1983), pp. 213-236.
[28] The accounts have been analysed by Patrice Beck (ed), *Vie de cour en Bourgogne à la fin du Moyen-Age* (Saint-Cyr-sur-Loire: Editions Sutton, 2002).
[29] Goehring (2020), pp. 335-36
[30] Gordon Kipling, *Enter the King: Theatre, Liturgy, and Ritual in the Medieval Civic Triumph* (Oxford: Oxford University Press, 1998), pp. 101-102.
[31] British Library, Cotton MSS, Vespasian B II, fol. 6r.
[32] Véronique Flammang and Marie van Eeeckenrode, 'Le jardinet de Hainaut: essai de typologie et clés d'interprétation (XIVe-XVIIIe siècles). Mises en scène d'un comet lors des inaugurations princières en Hainaut', *Bulletin de la Commission royale d'histoire,* 177 (2011), pp. 45-80 (p. 48); Margreet Brandsma, 'Lions or Lilies? The dynastic identity of Margaret of Burgundy (1374-1441) as represented by material objects', *Virtus,* 28 (2021), pp. 61-82 (p. 71).
[33] The lavish tomb of Mary of Burgundy in Bruges also showcases this iconography, breaking from the tradition of using 'pleurants' (crying figures) that had long dominated Burgundian Valois tomb design.
[34] See H. Th. Musper (ed), *Kaiser Maximilian's Weisskunig. In Lichtdruck-Faksimiles nach Frühdrucken mit Hilfe der Max Kade-Foundation, Inc.*, 2 vols. (Stuttgart: Verlag W. Kohlhammer, 1956), II: plates 66 and 67.
[35] Mechelen, Archief en Stadsbibliotheek MS s.s., fol. 1v.
[36] E. Bousmar, 'Maximilien d'Autriche ou le jeune Carles Quint? Enluminure et Politique dans le *Livre de Choeur* de Malines (1515)', in *Pour la Singulaire Affection qu'avons a luy: Études Bourguignonnes Offertes à Jean-Marie Cauchies*, Delsalle, ed by P. et al (Burgundica XXIV - Turnhout: Brepols, 2017), pp. 43-52; see also Goehring (2021), pp. 354-55.
[37] Goehring (2021), pp. 355-57
[38] For an overview of the history of the estate and its archaeology, see Vincent Heymans, Laetitia Cnockaert and Frédérique Honoré (eds), *Le Palais du Coudenberg à Bruxelles: du château médiéval au site archéologique* (Brussels: Coudenberg/Editions Mardaga, 2014).
[39] Brussels: Royal Museums of Fine Arts of Belgium inv. 2405, 2506; Goehring (2021), pp. 346-48.
[40] Brussels: City Museum MVB K-1941-1.
[41] Brussels: City Museum MVB K-1921-1
[42] For example, Claes Jansz Visscher in *Novissima et Accuratissima Leonis Belgici, seu Septemdecim Regionum Descriptio,* around 1611 (Brussels KBR, Kaarten en Plannen inv. Nr. 561-XIII a Pay-Bas Gen-1609-Visscher); Jan van de Velder II (after Bartholomeus de Mompere) in *Curia Brabantiae*, 1640 (British Museum 1840, 0314.169); and *Ducatus Brabantiae Nova Delineatio* published by Nicholas Visscher in 1656/1661 (Tilburg, Bib. Kath. Univ. Brabant, Brabant-Collectie, inv. Bo P67 n°81).

[43] E.A. Standen, *European Post-medieval Tapestries and Related Hangings in the Metropolitan Museum of Art*, 2 vols (New York: Metropolitan Museum of Art, 1985), i, pp. 308-315.

[44] Al Balis et al., *Les Chasses de Maximilien* (Paris: Réunion des musées nationaux, 1993).
[45] Yves Quairiaux, 'Mariemont à l'époque de Marie de Hongrie (1545-1554): L'Environnement paysager d'un domaine princier de campagne', in *Marie de Hongrie: politique et culture sous la renaissance aux Pays-Bas: Actes du colloque tenu au Musée royal de Mariemont les 11-12 Novembre 2005*, ed. by B. Federinov & G. Docquier (Mariemont: Musée Royal de Mariemont, 2008), pp. 191-192.
[46] Krista de Jonge, 'Marie de Hongrie, maître d'ouvrage (1531-1555), et la Renaissance dans les anciens Pays-Bas', in *Marie de Hongrie: politique et culture sous la renaissance aux Pays-Bas: Actes du colloque tenu au Musée royal de Mariemont les 11-12 Novembre 2005*, ed. by B. Federinov & G. Docquier (Mariemont: Musée Royal de Mariemont, 2008), pp. 136-39.
[47] Quairiaux (2008), p. 194.
[48] Cited by Quairiaux (2008), p. 198.
[49] On the three gardens at Binche, see Walter Cupperi, 'Sculptures et jardins dans le palais "à l'antique" de Binche: un programme iconographique précis?', in *Marie de Hongrie: politique et culture sous la renaissance aux Pays-Bas: Actes du colloque tenu au Musée royal de Mariemont les 11-12 Novembre 2005*, ed. by B. Federinov & G. Docquier (Mariemont: Musée Royal de Mariemont, 2008), p. 174-188 (pp. 180-183). The "grand jardin" seems to have also been called "le jardin nouveau emprès le posty" (see Cupperi (2008), p. 180), which has caused some confusion with the other "jardin nouveau" (cf. essay by Didier Dehon in the same volume).
[50] See Emily Peters, '1549 Knight's Game at Binche: Constructing Philip II's Ideal Identity in a Ritual of Honor', *Nederlands Kunsthistorisch Jaarboek* 49 (1998), pp. 10-35; Stijn Bussels, 'The Importance of Being Present: The Performances of Prince Philip in Binche and Antwerp' in *Charles V, Prince Philip, and the Politics of Succession: Imperial Festivities in Mons and Hainaut, 1549*, ed by M. McGowan and M. Shewring (European Festival Studies: 1450-1700 - Turnout: Brepols, 2020), pp. 157-78.
[51] Cupperi (2008).

5

CONVERSATIONS ACROSS CONTINENTS

Both papers in this chapter concern exchanges between Britain and Jamaica, one taking place in the heyday of the sugar cane – and slave - trade, the other in the 2020s. The first is the work of a local historian who explores how a Sussex family used their sugar fortunes in the late-eighteenth and early-nineteenth centuries to landscape their gardens and estate in modish and sometimes eccentric ways. The full title of the seminar series that inspired this chapter was 'Conversations across Continents: The Movement of Garden Styles, Ideas and Plants Across the Globe': however this paper brings in a new approach, focussing on how money made on one side of the Atlantic permitted horticultural extravaganza on the other.

The second paper hinges on a visit that a professor of Creative Writing in the UK makes to the rural heart of his Jamaican upbringing. It is not the result of research in archives, contemporary literature and later analyses like the other contributions in this volume: instead it is an account of a lived encounter with Jamaica's current and more distant horticultural story. More specifically, the focus is on healing plants: the author is caught between a western rationality and the possibility 'that Western science is not the *only* science that exists'. Linking both past and present is a trip to the hillside plot of a Jamaican herbalist who, like the plantation slaves before him, defies difficult terrain to grow his own and enjoy a sense of independence.[1] And looping back to Britain, a parallel is drawn between the tenacity of the herbalist and a Black man of Jamaican descent who farms a tiny holding in London.

[1] Lydia Mihelic Pulsipher, 'They have Saturdays and Sundays to Feed Themselves. Slave Gardens in the Caribbean', *Expedition*, Penn Museum, 32.2 (1990), pp 24-33.

FROM SUSSEX IRON TO JAMAICAN SUGAR: THE FULLERS OF ROSE HILL, SUSSEX

ALAN STARR

ABSTRACT

In recent years attention has increasingly focused on the English legacies of the slave trade with the houses and estates of those who had grown rich on sugar cane production in the West Indies coming in for scrutiny.[1] While grand properties such as Fonthill in Wiltshire and Harewood in Yorkshire might be prominent examples there are others such as Rose Hill in Brightling, near Robertsbridge in East Sussex, which merit investigation. Rose Hill was the home of the Fuller family for about two hundred years, from the late-seventeenth to the late-nineteenth century. The Fullers originally controlled a thriving iron business there but they also acquired plantations in Jamaica which, especially as the iron industry declined, were an enormous boost to their finances, making great changes to the gardens and wider landscape at Rose Hill possible in the eighteenth and early-nineteenth centuries.

INTRODUCTION

In a field near Wood's Corner, in what is now known as Brightling Park, East Sussex, stands a thirty five-foot high folly known as the Sugar Loaf because of its likeness to the sugar cones that were sold at the time it was built, in around the early nineteenth century (Figure 1).

Figure 1. The Sugar Loaf, Brightling. Photo: Alan Starr (2019)

Although supposedly constructed to resemble the spire of the nearby church of St Giles at Dallington,[2] it stands as a testimony to the source of the funds which made it possible for several generations of the Fuller family to develop and enhance the gardens and wider landscape at their Rose Hill home. This paper looks at how from first building up wealth from the very local iron industry the Fullers would come to rely increasingly on an inter-continental business, namely sugar cane production in, and exports from, Jamaica, the island that became England's most important supplier. For several decades there were rich rewards which coincided with lavish spending at Rose Hill, evidence of which can still to be seen today.

IRONMASTERS IN THE SUSSEX WEALD

The Fuller family first became wealthy as ironmasters in the Sussex Weald. From Roman times there had been small-scale bloomeries here, producing pig-iron. Then, in 1490, the blast-furnace arrived in Sussex. The Weald, with its ironstone, timber and running water, had all of the ingredients needed for an iron industry. At the beginning of the seventeenth century, the historian William Camden described the region thus:

> It is full of Iron-mines everywhere; for the casting of which, there are Furnaces up and down the Country; and abundance of wood is yearly spent; many streams are drawn into one Channel, and a great deal of meadow-ground is turned into Ponds and Pools, for the driving of Mills by the flashes; which beating with hammers upon the iron, fill the neighbourhood round about, night and day, with their noise. . . the Proprietors of the mines, by casting of Cannon and other things, get a great deal of money.[3]

Having taken out a lease on a foundry in 1650, built a blast-furnace at Heathfield in 1691 and acquired a forge at Burwash, the Fullers were among those still getting a 'great deal of money' a century later as, among other things, they turned iron into cannons, some of them thirty-two pounders, ten-foot long and of the highest quality. Today the estate still has a statue of a cannon and flames, cast in iron (Figure 2).

Figure 2. Statue in Brightling Park. Photo: Alan Starr (2018)

By the end of the seventeenth century some of the Fullers' products were being carried well beyond Europe. In 1700 the slaver *Henrietta Marie* left London, armed with Fuller cannon. Its route took it first to West Africa, then on to Jamaica where 191 Africans were put on sale. On the third leg of its triangular journey, off the coast of Florida, it sank.[4] When the wreck was investigated the Fuller guns were discovered, along with some iron shackles which would be very unlikely to have come from the Weald.

ROSE HILL AND NEW SUGAR WEALTH

With money derived from the iron industry Thomas Fuller (1655-1720) acquired land at Brightling on which he had a new house built around 1697 (Figure 3). He later gave the house and its twenty three acres to his nephew John Fuller (1680-1745) who changed its name to Rose Hill in honour of his wife, Elizabeth Rose (1681-1728). Importantly, for the future of the family, Elizabeth was the daughter of Fulke Rose (1644-1694), one of the first men to start great sugar fortunes in Jamaica in the late 1660s and early 1670s.[5] By the 1680s he was already earning over £4,000 a year from his plantations and when his daughter married John Fuller in 1703 she brought money and just over 3,000 acres of Rose's land into the family.[6] She also brought strong botanical links with her, as her widowed mother, also Elizabeth (d. 1724) had married Hans Sloane (1660-1753) in 1695. Elizabeth Fuller's eldest son used to write to his grandfather on matters of natural history and her second son followed Sloane into a medical career and out to the West Indies.[7]

Figure 3. J.M.W Turner, watercolour of 'Rosehill', Sussex, J.M.W. Turner, 1816. Courtesy of British Museum

Although he might have had greater financial resources, there is not much evidence of John Fuller I being interested in the grounds at Rose Hill, other than perhaps investing in new exotic plants, some of which he acquired from Philip Miller, the chief gardener at the Chelsea Physic Garden, and others possibly from the famous nurseryman Thomas Fairchild of Hoxton. He also asked his son Rose Fuller (see below) to send him 'curious' seeds for the garden from Leiden where the latter was studying medicine at the time; but he feared that they would have to be entered at the Custom House, and be caught up in government bureaucracy.[8] However, great changes were to come about after his son, another John (1706-1755), inherited in 1745. Year by year this John extended the property from its original twenty three acres, eventually owning a consolidated park of 242 acres. He created a deer park and built a Chinese temple within it.[9] Anxious to give the house greater privacy, he closed off the public road which ran beside it, building a new one a respectable distance away. [10]

Despite adding substantially to the estate and extending the house by creating a stylish western wing, and even attiring some of his servants in livery, John Fuller II was curiously anxious about his finances. The iron industry might not have been as successful as before but the local landholdings were profitable, and there was another source of money: the family plantations in Jamaica whose returns had been greatly increased by the presence of John's eldest brother, Rose (1708-1777). Having trained as a doctor in Leiden, Rose was sent out to the West Indies in 1733 and was soon the manager of the family's sugar estates.[11] At that point, beset by mismanagement and a fall in prices, the sugar estates were bringing in only about £300 a year but by the 1750s the plantations were giving John Fuller II £1,000 a year; the ironworks yielded £2,000, local landholdings gave £1,200 and he earned £600 from other investments. [12]

Rising sugar prices helped boost the family's income. In addition Rose Fuller acquired new land – and slaves – on his own account and when in 1737 he married the sixteen-year-old Ithamar Mill, daughter of Jamaica's chief justice and a wealthy plantation owner, he acquired another sizeable plantation and 140 slaves.[13] By 1754 he owned a total of 1,501 acres of land in St Catherine and St Thomas-in-the-Vale, as well as a share of another 646 acres in St Catherine.[14] He became deeply involved in Jamaica: he was very active in the island's politics, which proved a drain on the family resources, and also had a long-standing relationship with his 'housekeeper' Mary Rose, a healer of mixed ancestry.[15]

Rose Fuller inherited Rose Hill on his brother's death in 1755, at which point he returned to England, and to the family home where he, like his brother before him, took an interest in the estate. A visitor to Rose Hill in 1768 saw him 'as busily employed in the sowing of turnips, raising of corn and improving his land here, as he was formerly in the planting of sugar canes.'[16] Regarding the park, he was possibly following recommendations from Capability Brown who, in the 1760s and 1770s was working on the transformation of the grounds at nearby Ashburnham Place.[17] Rose visited Ashburnham at this time and we know from Humphry Repton that Brown made some suggestions as, in the Red Book he made for Rose Hill (see below), he wrote, somewhat disparagingly:

> No plan on paper can be so accurate and minute as to supercede [sic] the necessity of marking the detail for execution on the spot. This is evident from some parts of Mr Brown's plan having been misunderstood while others have fortunately not been adopted ...[18]

This remark does not, obviously, give any clue as to which of Brown's suggestions might have been acted upon, even if not as Brown had actually intended. There, is, though, a strong indication that his ideas had had some impact on how Rose Hill was developed.

'MAD' JACK FULLER AND THE FLOURISHING OF ROSE HILL

When Rose died in 1777 he was succeeded by his nephew, twenty-year-old Jack Fuller (1757-1834). Jack had been to Eton and enrolled at Lincoln's Inn, but had no career, or need of one since he was a very rich young man. Jack was a wildly eccentric but jovial squire, a man of both boorish behaviour and sophisticated tastes. He frequented London's fashionable circles, but rewarded outsiders: the post of Fullerian Professor of Chemistry was established specifically to give security to Michael Faraday. He was also a patron of Turner who painted various views in the area around Rose Hill including one of the Observatory (see below), which includes at its centre 'the gardener's house embosomed amidst rich and elegant trees' (Figure 4).[19]

When Jack inherited his fortune in 1777, the local iron industry was failing as the Midlands and Scotland now produced cannon which surpassed the Wealden guns on cost and quality. The Heathfield foundry began to close in 1787 and in 1803 Jack Fuller sold the declining forge at Burwash.[20]

Although the local iron industry might have been in decline, Jack Fuller was still able to spend money lavishly, helped by revenues from the sugar plantations.[21] In 1797, perhaps to mark the centenary of the house, the cartographers Russell and Gream mapped his estate and in March 1806 there was a visit from Humphry Repton, who provided one of his famous Red Books (which is held today by the Bodleian Library). It is a 'muted affair' that includes a map and illustrates some possible changes to the house and gardens. [22]

Figure 4. W.B. Cooke after J.M.W. Turner, Brightling Observatory seen from Rosehill Park, 1816, Tate Gallery. Creative Commons CC-BY-NC-ND (3.0 Unported)

There are also some suggestions regarding the wider park where Repton proposed building a temple as a focal point, on a rounded hill which he called the 'Knoll'.[23] These minor improvements were not his main concern, however. His real interest was more radical: he felt that the house was in an exposed position and needed to be rebuilt in a more sheltered location in the park. Repton returned to

Rose Hill in the autumn of 1806 but it seems the visit resulted in acrimony, possibly because there was no agreement on resiting the house. Repton wrote to Fuller the following March saying:

> I must observe that as there is nothing more mortifying to a professional Man than to deliver an opinion which he knows is not to be acted upon; so I cannot but regret, the little use of my Visits...'[24]

However, while his plans for the house may have come to nothing, some of Repton's suggestions - notably the construction of a second carriageway across the estate - were acted upon, although it is not clear that Repton himself had a part in this. There were other changes too that had a distinctly Reptonian ring about them. For example Repton had proposed that a straight belt of trees be broken up with projecting clumps of trees, something which appears to have been done very quickly after his visit. And although he might later have changed his mind about its siting, the construction of a Grecian temple on top of Repton's 'Knoll' went ahead.[25]

With or without the advice of Humphry Repton it is obvious that Jack Fuller was anxious to have the best for the gardens at Rose Hill. In the *Gentleman's Quarterly* of 1788, there is a notice of the death of Mr. Close, his gardener, 'remarkable for his skill in the management of hot-houses'.[26] Rose Hill had a large walled kitchen garden of nearly two acres, and its hot-houses were an important feature. In 1826 a newspaper reported that the head gardener Mr Taylor had some extraordinary melons, thirty-three inches in diameter 'and of exquisite flavour'.[27]

AN ARRAY OF FOLLIES

While Jack Fuller may have been a follower of fashion in some of his landscaping he was certainly not afraid to make a very personal and individual mark on the estate, specifically in the follies for which Rose Hill, now renamed Brightling Park, is renowned. There is perhaps a link between West Indian cash and follies: Beckford's Fonthill Abbey is contemporaneous with Fuller's more modest constructions.

Some of Jack Fuller's early works at Rose Hill are amateurish. There is a summerhouse of brick, faced with assembled Coade stone, dated 1803. This looks west across the park in the rough direction of the so-called Sugar Loaf, already mentioned. The summerhouse has been attributed to Robert Smirke (1780-1867) but it predates his career as an architect. Similarly, the crudely built Sugar Loaf is unlikely to have been the work of an architect of any kind.[28]

The other monuments which punctuate the park and surrounding land bear witness to an eclectic or eccentric taste. They certainly give few clues as to the date or meaning of their construction. For example there is a statue of the Greek hunter Meleager and his dog, which could possibly be related to the rabies outbreak of 1813, which caused Jack to put down his pet spaniels. There is an iron statue of a cannon, a flame and an anchor; it is thought locally to celebrate the Battle of the Nile which took place in 1798 but may, as already mentioned, be merely a reference to the Fuller family's gun-making business (Figure 2). Similarly, an Egyptian-style obelisk at the top of Brightling Beacon, was possibly built to celebrate the victory over Napoleon at Waterloo in 1815, although alternative theories abound.

While it is doubtful that Robert Smirke had anything to do with the summerhouse or the Sugar Loaf, it can be assumed that he was responsible for the pyramid built in Brightling churchyard as Fuller's mausoleum, the proportions of which are the same as those of the pyramid of Cestius in Rome which Smirke would doubtless have seen while on the Grand Tour. He certainly built the Greek temple on the hill in the park which has already been mentioned and was once the site of a windmill (Figure 5). There was another windmill to the north-west of the park, which was replaced after 1810 by Smirke's Observatory. This was not apparently intended to be a decorative structure, but, in keeping with Jack Fuller's scientific interests, was equipped with equatorial and zenith telescopes.[29]

Figure 5. Robert Smirke's Temple at Brightling. Photo: Alan Starr (2018)

DEFENDING SLAVERY

Jack Fuller died in April 1834 just a few months before the Abolition of Slavery Act came into effect in August that year. He had been an implacable opponent of abolition which he, like other plantation owners, believed would harm not only the sugar industry but also the economy more generally. His views on slavery were not nuanced. He argued that the British poor were treated worse than his slaves. In fact, he felt that his slaves were very lucky to have him as a master. He was reported as saying:

> Slavery was no particular hardship upon the Negroes. He declared that he felt no remorse whatever in having such men on his estate, particularly as they were generally well treated, and had the opportunity of purchasing their freedom by industry.[30]

There are distinct echoes of Jack Fuller's stance in *A Descriptive Account of the Island of Jamaica*[31] written in 1790 by William Beckford, one of the island's largest plantation owners. The two volumes, which included 'observations' on the consequence of abolishing the slave trade and emancipating slaves, put forward such claims as that the slaves' work was less arduous than that of peasants in England, that their houses were possibly better than those in poorer, more remote parts of England and that they had more time off than many of the poor in England. This time off, which was every Sunday and some Saturdays, could hardly be described as 'leisure time', though, as many slaves used it to tend their 'grounds', the plots, often in difficult mountainous terrain, where they grew fruit and vegetables for their families and for the market.

There is very little to suggest that Rose Fuller, the only member of the Rose Hill family to visit Jamaica, had seen things differently. Having become actively involved in the politics of the island, where he was appointed to the Supreme Court, he hoped to get the job of Agent for the Jamaica Assembly when this became vacant in 1764. In the event the post was given to his brother Stephen (1716-1799) whose remit was to lobby in London to further the trade interests of the Jamaican planters. He persuaded the Royal Navy to give up its traditional brandy and to replace it with West Indian rum. He ensured that the poorhouses of England were given large volumes of molasses, purchased by the government.[32] In the last decades of the century, he became more involved in fighting the Abolitionists. Rose, who was MP for Rye from 1756-1777, supported his brother fully, and became well known for his sympathies. When a bookseller sought to promote a print of a placid Jamaican scene, he wisely dedicated it to Rose Fuller (Figure 6).

Figure 6. Anon, *A View of the Dry Harbour in the Parish of St Ann's Jamaica*, anon, 1769, dedicated to Rose Fuller; Library of Congress, Wikimedia commons

A large proportion of Rose Fuller's Jamaican wealth was made up of slaves: when he died his estate in Jamaica was valued at around £22,000 in Jamaican currency, of which £18,000 was attributable to enslaved people.[33] He had prided himself on foregoing any unnecessary cruelty in his approach to his slaves, claiming that this had helped him turn round the profitability of the family's sugar estates. Even so, we see that one apprehended slave called Hector was 'the property of Rose Fuller and marked RF'. The same initials which would be stamped into the trunions of Fuller cannon.[34]

Rose Fuller and other planters might have considered that the slave's lot was not such an unhappy one, and could be ameliorated by humane treatment, but the fact remains that they were regarded as chattels. This was more than apparent in Rose Fuller's will where a legacy to his erstwhile housekeeper in Jamaica included six slaves. [35]

A CHANGED LANDSCAPE FOR ROSE HILL

However much the Fullers might have resisted it, the abolition of slavery was inevitable, but in fact there were other factors working against a sustained income stream from their holdings in Jamaica. On the one hand there were intermittent wars, as well as slave uprisings, disease and natural disasters; on the other, competition from new cane producing territories and, by the 1820s, from a burgeoning sugar beet industry in Europe. Jamaica's sugar exports fell from 100,000 tons in 1805 to 20,000 a year for much of the rest of the century and with it the number of plantations shrank too.[36] The deterioration in the Wealden iron industry has already been noted and, even though he may have received a generous legacy from Jack Fuller (who left £160,000 to two heirs) as well as payments of over £4,500 under the compensation for slaves scheme that formed part of the Abolition of Slavery Act,[37] Fuller's heir Augustus Elliott Fuller (1777-1857) appears to have taken a financially cautious stance with regard to his new estate. A map of Rose Hill in 1840 suggests that the focus was moving more towards the productive. There were still gardens, including a kitchen garden, a fruit garden, a flower garden and a melon ground, but the circular ornamental pond, which once stood to the north of the house, was emptied and converted to a pheasantry.[38] A new pond was constructed to the south of the kitchen garden, not as an ornament but to power a sawmill: Augustus also hoped to use the water to power a threshing machine and to cut gorse.[39]

However, the grounds still appear to have been kept in good order. Although, when he visited in 1842, John Claudius Loudon might have been critical of the state of the woodland, he had praise for the gardener, Mr Ogle, who kept the kitchen garden, and 'formed near it some beautiful ornamental scenery'. [40] Rose Hill was put up for sale in 1879, bringing to an end nearly two centuries of ownership by the Fullers and the name of Rose Hill, which now changed to Brightling Park. The sales particulars proclaimed that the 'park was laid out and planted during the last century with much taste by a distinguished landscape gardener and its sylvan beauties are now fully developed.'[41] There can be little doubt that these beauties would not have existed but for sugar riches, and the slave labour that made them possible.

REFERENCES

[1] See, for example, Matthew Parker, *The Sugar Barons,* (London: Bloomsbury, 2011), and Madge Dresser and Andrew Hann, eds., *Slavery and the British Country House* (Swindon: English Heritage, 2013).

[2] On the Sugar Loaf and other follies built in the grounds of Rose Hill, now Brightling Park, see Annette Lloyd Thomas, *Mad Jack: The Many Lives of John Fuller, Squire of Brightling* (Robertsbridge: Otherwise-Publishing, 2020), pp. 147-163.

[3] William Camden, *Britannia,* translated by Edmund Gibson (London: Printed by Mary Matthews for Awnsham Churchill, 1772), p. 196.

[4] https://www.floridaslavetradecenter.org/Gallery/24 [accessed 16/02/2023].

[5] Calendar of State Papers, Colonial 1669-74, n.270.

[6] Calendar of State Papers, Colonial 1681-5, n. 1553, 25 February 1684; David Crossley and Richard Saville, *The Fullers Letters: Guns, Slaves and Finances, 1728-1755* (Lewes: Sussex Record Society, 1991), pp. xxiv, xxv.

[7] M.C.L. Salt, 'The Fullers of Brighton Park III', *Sussex Archaeological Collections*, no.107, (Lewes: Sussex Archaeological Society, 1969), p. 23.

[8] Crossley and Saville, pp. 14, 20, 33. For more on Philip Miller see, for example, William T. Stearn, 'Philip Miller and the plants from the Chelsea Physic Garden presented to the Royal Society of London, 1723–1796', *Transactions of the Botanical Society of Edinburgh*, 41:3 (1972), pp. 293-307; on Thomas Fairchild see Michael Leapman, *The Ingenious Mr Fairchild, The Forgotten Father of the Flower Garden* (London: Headline, 2000).
[9] David and Barbara Martin, Tenement analysis – Brightling, c.1990, held by East Sussex Records Office, Ref. HBR 9/8.
[10] Salt, 'The Fullers of Brighton Park III', pp.14-15.
[11] 'Rose Fuller MP of Jamaica and Rose Hill', *Profile and Legacies Summary*, Centre for the Study of the Legacies of British Slavery, University College London.
[12] M.W. McCahill ed, *The correspondence of Stephen Fuller: 1788-1795: Jamaica, the West India interest at Westminster, and the campaign to preserve the slave trade* (London: Wiley-Blackwell for the Parliamentary History Yearbook Trust, 2014), p. 27.
[13] Crossley and Saville, pp. xxv-vi, 103.
[14] 'Rose Fuller MP of Jamaica and Rose Hill Sussex', Centre for the Study of the Legacies of British Slavery.
[15] M.C.L. Salt, 'The Fullers of Brighton Park II', *Sussex Archaeological Collections*, no.106, (Lewes: Sussex Archaeological Society, 1968), p. 75; Letters from Mary Rose to Rose Fuller, held by East Sussex Records Office, SAS/FR 21.
[16] Anne M. Powers, *A Parcel of Ribbons* (Raleigh, North Carolina: Lulu.com, 2012), p. 116.
[17] Alan and Jennie Starr, 'Brightling Park' in *'Capability' Brown in Sussex*, ed. by Susi Batty (Sussex Gardens Trust, 2016), pp. 16-7.
[18] Alan and Jennie Starr, 'Brightling Park' in *'Capability' Brown in Sussex*, ed. by Susi Batty (Sussex Gardens Trust, 2016), p. 16.
[19] 'Fine Arts', *The Examiner for Year* 1819 (London: John Hunt, 1819), p. 508.
[20] Kate Mees, 'Documentary and literary evidence relating to Burwash Forge and Wynhamford Mill, East Sussex' in *Wealden Iron*, Vol.30, (Wealden Iron Research Group, 2010), p. 22.
[21] See the Account Book, Rosehill, 1797 – 1817, held by East Sussex Records Office SAS/RF 15/45 to indicate the value of the sugar reaching England.
[22] Alan and Jennie Starr, 'Rose Hill: the mansion of a British senator' in *Humphry Repton in Sussex*, ed. by Susi Batty (Sussex Gardens Trust, 2018), pp. 96-105 (p.96).
[23] Starr and Starr, 'Rose Hill: the mansion of a British senator', p. 102.
[24] Humphry Repton, *Red Book for Rose Hill, Sussex,* 1806 (held at the Bodleian Library) quoted in Starr and Starr, 'Rose Hill: the mansion of a British senator', p. 97.
[25] ibid, p. 103-4.
[26] *The Gentleman's Magazine and Historical Chronicle*, (London, 1788), p. 367.
[27] *The Sussex Advertiser* (31 August 1826), p. 2.
[28] Starr and Starr, 'Rose Hill: the mansion of a British senator', pp. 100-1.
[29] 'Observatories: Sussex', *Survey of Astronomical History,* Blog atWordPress.com [accessed 2 March 2023].
[30] *The London Chronicle* (14 June 1804), p. 4.
[31] William Beckford, *A Descriptive Account of the Island of Jamaica*, 2 vols (London: printed for T. and J. Egerton, 1790), ii, pp.66, 20, 137, 151—3, 155.
[32] Parker, Chapter 25, Kindle ebook, p. 301.
[33] 'Rose Fuller MP of Jamaica and Rose Hill', Centre for the Study of the Legacies of British Slavery.
[34] *Royal Gazette of Jamaica* (10 November 1781), p. 12.
[35] See Linda L. Sturtz, 'Mary Rose: "White" African Jamaican Woman? Race and Gender in Eighteenth-Century Jamaica' in *Gendering the African Diaspora: Women, Culture, and Historical Change in the Caribbean and Nigerian Hinterland,* ed. by Judith A. Byfield, LaRay Denzer and Anthea Morrison (Indiana: Indiana University Press, 2012) pp. 59-87, (p. 64).
[36] Parker, Chapter 29, Kindle ebook, p. 355, Epilogue, p. 358.
[37] 'Augustus Elliott Fuller', *Profile and Legacies Summary*, Centre for the Study of the Legacies of British Slavery.
[38] See Map of Rosehill Park in Brightling and Dallington, c. 1840, held by East Sussex Records Office, SAS/RF 15/12/1, contrasted with the map of the Park in Repton's Red Book.
[39] *The North Wales Chronicle* (30 May 1848), p. 4.
[40] John Claudius Loudon, 'Notice of Some Gardens and Country Seats in Sussex, visited in October 1842', *The Gardener's Magazine,* 1842, p. 615.
[41] *The Globe* (10 July 1877), p. 8.

PLANT TELEGRAPHY: DREAMS AND CONVERSATIONS

JASON ALLEN-PAISANT

ABSTRACT

A walk in English woodland recalls earlier walks and conversations in search of plants in Jamaica. The plants are medicinal and the search directed as much by dreams as knowledge, tradition and a long and close relationship with the local flora. These same elements shine through in an encounter with a rasta herbalist in Jamaica in more recent times.

MEMORIES AND DREAMS

During the COVID pandemic, my emotional home is Coffee Grove, Jamaica, where the woodland is aware and conversational. Physically, I'm in Leeds, where walking in the woods is like learning a new language, like having a second first experience of the world, or, as V. S. Naipaul's West Indian protagonist characterizes his experience of the English countryside in *The Enigma of Arrival*, a 'second childhood of seeing'.[1] Connecting with the woods in Yorkshire affords me imaginative journeys back to the woodlands of Coffee Grove.

Images come to me now of my grandmother walking through the woodlands. It's early morning, and the dew is still on the grass. First, we walk along beaten footpaths, then gradually move through rough grassland, as Mama (this is what I call my grandmother) clears a way through tall bushes with a stick. She's looking for three specific herbs. She does not remember the names of all three. They were 'given to her in a dream'—she needs to make a tea with them to cure her cough that's now developing into bronchitis. She remembers the name, and the very character, of two (sarsaparilla, John Charles)—she's deeply acquainted with these plants—but if she's walking and looking like this—slowly, moving the grass with her stick, craning the neck, bending—it's because scanning the bush like this will help her recall what the third one was. Plants have power, and we depend on them; this is self-evident, a knowledge carried in our bodies—a kind of archive passed down from generation to generation—so this way of walking and looking, practised by the grown-ups here—not just Mama—conveys a deep awareness of the powers that the plants have.

I consider now the way she walked, which had everything to do with the way she looked at the land that surrounded her. She would walk with one arm gripping the other behind her back, the way Jamaican 'country people' do, while examining the bush. It was an engaged way of looking around; it had so much familiarity in it, but what it had most was a sort of expectation. I have probably never thought about this before now, and it must have always seemed normal to me, this way of hers, which was the way of many people in the district. The old woman whose property abutted our own also walked in the same way. In my mind's eye, I see this body language in everyone who ever walked in the bush in Coffee Grove.

My grandmother would often have woken up with a dream on her mind. The dream was about specific herbs she needed to collect—it was always three or five, odd numbers; according to tradition, the number should never be even. I've never heard the reason behind this, nor know anyone who has;

it has always been *just so*, and the belief has exerted a fascination on my imagination, a curiosity for practices from whose sources we have been disconnected.

Mama needed to gather the particular herbs revealed to her in her dream, to boil them and make a tea. One of us might have been ill, and the dream revealed the precise concoction she needed to make to cure us. As she looked around while walking, she may have been scanning the bush to remember the particular ones she was given in the dream, or to remember which one or ones she'd forgotten. One could never be sure as she would never reveal the precise contents of her dream until she had performed the acts that it solicited. This is also tradition.

We used many herbs in our home back then. As a child, I grew to know their uses. *Fever grass* was evidently for fever, and only when I moved to England did I learn that it was, in fact, called 'lemon grass' by the English and other people, who also use it for its healing properties. I still find magic, however, in our naming of herbs based on their therapeutic or medicinal uses, as it seems to reveal something about our thinking and our history. Naming is storytelling, and that form of naming betokens its own particular relationship to the plant. From a certain point of view, that relationship may seem reductive in its emphasis on the plant's utility, but in another sense, it's a relationship of proximity and intimacy, one that conveys a sense of vulnerability, for knowing this grass as *fever grass* is also an expression of dependence. Here, particularly in the countryside, people care very little about English or European botanical names or Latin classifications. As if to highlight that fact, and to subvert the European names, Jamaicans have also conferred English plant names onto local ones which may be radically different in appearance and identity from the English one. For us, dandelion is an aromatic shrub that grows seeds in a long, slender pod. The only thing suggestive of the dandelions that constellate every springtime in Roundhay Park, Leeds, is the yellowness of their small flowers; not even the shape is the same. Sage, marigold, and plantain, among others, have had similar fortunes.

Jointa is a herb that has almost fallen out of my memory. I remember loving the pungent odour it released upon being broken; I could taste it. Right now, I'm trying to conjure the spicy quality of its smell. As a child, I imagined that *jointa* was associated with the joints of the body and used for associated complaints. In my mind, the name followed the same logic as *fever grass*, as *search mi heart*. The latter conveyed more mystery, however, as I grew up in the devoutly religious environment of the village, with its Church of God, in which Anglo-Saxon Protestantism blended with African gestural repertoires and music. The African element constantly sought to free itself and express a spirituality of its own, but was always restrained, tempered, by a corporeality that was different from it, more 'respectable'. Growing up in strict religious environments is the reality of a great many Jamaicans of country and of town, but the closed atmosphere of the hamlet, which seemed unaware of any other people except its own, intensified this devoutness. The community had only itself as reference, since people seldom travelled outside of the district in those days. The elders and the bible were our only morality. Things were slightly looser for people who had the privilege of going to school – my mother had been one of those. It was precisely *because* of her schooling that I spent my early years with my grandmother. She was at teachers' college at the time, and had me somewhere in the middle, I reckon, of her time there. She was twenty-one years old when I was born, a naïve young girl who must have never had a boyfriend until she fell upon my father, whom, to this day, I have not met.

Growing up with my grandmother, I perceived herbal medicine to be a natural part of our everyday life. To say *perceived* may be inaccurate, since one never thought about such things, one simply lived them; we lived with plants—with our bushes, the name we gave herbs. I've lost the names of many of them now, but a few of the fascinating ones return, which also happen to be some of the ones my mother gives to me, packed in Ziploc bags, each time I'm returning to England from a trip home. *Search mi heart* made me think not only of the physical heart—I imagined the properties of the weed moving through and inspecting the cardiac ventricles while the individual slept—but also of that spiritual inner place, the elusive one, which we refer to as 'the heart', and I wondered, then, why people should want to associate the idea of spiritual cleansing with a plant. It makes much more sense to me now.

Already, I was fascinated by the names left behind for things; they were relics and remnants of an event or of a particular revelation—they are the residues of the stories that are within them. Take the bush called *John Charles*, for instance. Who was he and how did he come to have an entire plant named after him among our people? Other bushes follow the logic of medicinal or pharmacopaeic usage, sometimes comically. Consider *inflation weed* for instance. Knowing the bawdy humour of our ancestors, I assume now that *inflation weed* may refer, mockingly, to the problem of impotence which it is meant to treat. Other bush names are less 'indicative', but the names have no less a sense of vernacular poetry: *leaf of life, Guinea hen weed, strong back, sarsaparilla, chainy root, Jack in the Bush*.

But this issue of names of bushes and of the intimacies they convey relates very much to my peasant people's way of walking. It strikes me that knowing the woodland like this means that one is not a passive walker. For Mama, Mammy, and so many farmers and dwellers in Coffee Grove, knowledge of trees and plants was not just scientific. What was significant about trees and bushes was not merely the rationality of why we need them; the need to engage with them was equally, if not more, important, and I saw that engagement every day, in so many forms. There was a kind of respect shown towards the woodlands.

*****

CONVERSING WITH CONGOLIN

It's day six of my trip to Jamaica. After walking for more than an hour I'm tired; I sit on the spore-like rock of a karst hillside; my backside is uncomfortable. I'm happy to enjoy a bit of rest while Congolin, a herbalist rasta I've befriended, goes off to help his farmer brethren retrieve a thousand-dollar note lost somewhere on this hill. I met Congolin yesterday in the street in Mount Pleasant. *A dis a di man yu need fi talk to!,* Maas Owen had declared, his eyes beaming, as he used his head to point to Congolin, a short, skinny rastaman with friendly eyes and a permanently affixed smile. When I meet him, he's wearing a small backpack, which I imagine might contain herbs, as I stand along the roadside listening to him speak to the group of men gathered there—myself, Maas Owen, a certain Mr. Lee, Maas Owen's friend, Damion and his son, another rasta man. The men listen attentively and with respect to the authoritative medicine man. Knowledge pours out of him about all sorts of plants, ones I had known and others about which I had no clue; plants whose uses I'd heard about and others whose virtues I'd never suspected;

the things he's managed to do that have baffled even the doctors. But above all, what strikes me is the *way* he talks about plants—with love, as if they were darlings. *Eternal Father, Divine Mother, please give me the blessing and the gift to hear from the plants...* is a prayer he formulates every morning. *The woman have a lot to play, you can't leave har outta di concept,* he clarifies: for him, God is male and female. He mentions that the plants whisper to him, and I want to know exactly what this feels and looks like. He explains that it involves feeling the joy of the plants, entering into a sort of empathy with them in which he can feel and understand their emotions. *Plants have feelings*, he insists, *you have to understand them if you goin use them; you can't just use them based on your selfish longings; you haffi really love the plants them if you want them fi work. The plants them don't give the same power every day and the same time every day.* In his statements, what I find clarifying is that being a herbalist involves recognizing that the plants are communicative. If I've instinctively felt this since I was a child growing up with Mama, this is something I was never taught in my biology classes in high school. In fact, it seems to go against those lessons. Some might denounce this sort of thinking as anti-science, but this is the basis of Congolin's practice, and of an entire relationship to plants—for him, who leans into it to such a high degree, but also for all those in the community who turn to him because of their beliefs. I would never discount the insights provided by Western science, which have been of tremendous value, but is it possible to entertain the idea that plants also seek to communicate with us? This might mean entertaining the notion that Western science is not the *only* science that exists.

As Congolin returns to the top of the hill, he takes a seat beside me, cotching himself on one of the rocks. I ask him questions about when he began to perceive his gift of hearing from the plants. According to him, one day in 1972:

> *a lightening take me up more than your height off the ground, hang me up in the air for more than ten or twenty minutes...From yasso a mi shoulder down to mi heel, it black and blue, scortch up. It happen pon the mountain ova desso. A brother was there, and him run left me go outta road and tell people say me dead. When I go home, I say, I naa go a no doctor. And a from them time deh some tings start happen to me.*

Rationality is hard to abandon. Yet, there are stories all around the world of people who've discovered miraculous giftings after being struck by lightning. According to my mother, lightning might have held him in the air for ten seconds, which might have seemed like ten minutes, but even that is hard to imagine.

The plant them whisper to me. I can't deny that that bit of Western rationalism ingrained in me by my education remains. Besides, I've heard so many stories here and there about plant whisperers; the phenomenon has become something of a modern-day legend. It seems like an easy narrative thread to pull on. But I'm also from a community of people among whom there are vestigial traces of animism. This *also* is something that's part of my upbringing, even if it's been silenced over the years by my Western education—the belief that so-called inanimate things can speak, that our people listen to them, can hear them speak. I believe in the communicative qualities of matter, and that it too, like us, consists of energy, and communicates in felt ways. This is why I listen to Congolin. *What does the whisper sound like, how exactly do the plants whisper to you?,* I ask. The answer he gives is not particularly clarifying—*You have a complaint or a sickness within you, and I ask the Father for the knowledge, to open my blind eyes*. His stories, as well as his answers, are very digressive; it's hard to pin him down to a straight answer to any question. *I always give thanks to Father,* he continues, saying:

> *Give thanks for your great concept of healing'. This a something me pray for you know, me ask Father fi bless me with great healing concep' of herbs fi heal the sickness in me. Then one of the time me get a vision, a me Auntie me vision see and she show me one bush—me have certain sickness—and say fi use this bush, and if it good fi me, it good fi others. And me use up the bush, rub it pon me; anywhere me a feel pain, the pain dimmish.*

Many stories of healing involve an episode such a this, in which a dead loved-one *dreams* the sick person and reveals to them what herbs they need to use and, as often happens, how. This dream might be the result of 'prayer'. But it does seem that prayer may be broadly conceived here, not as necessarily a request to the Christian God, but as a request to his ancestors and to the plants themselves. Indeed, Congolin suggests that the 'prayer' may not be verbalized as actual words, but that he reaches out to the divine being through the intensity of his yearning. Often, it's this attentiveness and this yearning, more powerful and precise than words, that are reciprocated in the form of a dream. Is this bad science? Maybe. But Congolin's practice is based on a system, which might be closer to Jamaican *siyans* than to Western science. His science has meaning; it also has a history, if a largely unwritten one.

Meanwhile, along the roadside, as we descend the hill, he takes pleasure in naming the bushes. I am realising both how many I already know and how many there are to discover. It seems we could spend the entire afternoon on the road like this, because almost every bush has an identity, even if it has no name that can be found in a book. Now, he points to the *jackana bush*, aka 'Jack in the Bush', recounting how he's used it to treat prostate cancer. Now he points to donkey weed. *All this a medicine you know, it powerful so till*—pointing to a pomegranate tree. When he points out *memory weed* to me, I realise that it's the same herb I've encountered in England as *rosemary*. It's the very same plant. It's a pleasure to share like this, and for each bush, there are multiple stories— of healings, within one's family, of an individual one knows, of someone one hears about, of a legend—and dreams. Always the dreams. Dreams, healing, and herbs: they work together.

In Jamaica, there's a particular kind of dream known as a vision. Some, like Congolin, differentiate 'vision' from 'dream'. According to him, a vision is when *something come clear to you—a same so you see it, a so it go*; whereas a dream *don't walk straight, you haffi interpret it. Vision a the thing that you see and it come tru quick.* It's in the morning when he's about to wake up that visions generally come to him, he explains. He describes himself at these moments as being in a liminal state, neither quite awake nor quite asleep, so that he's conscious of everything happening around. In fact, he adds that he is as if out of his body, looking down at himself; he can see himself lying on the bed. *That is when the plants come to talk to me*. Perhaps he merely hears their voice, while seeing images of what plants he is to pick, images of the people (friends, family) that they are for, etc. He's not in this as a business. He lives a very simple lifestyle in the small house which he shares with a sister, and he walks everywhere—miles. I can see that this is a man much more into helping people than into money, and if those people find it in their consciences—he does hope that they do—to offer him some money as a thank-you, then he's grateful. For him, this gift of visions and the *great knowledge of whispering sound,* as he often refers to it, are things to be shared around rather than sold. *Them say me mad,* he continues, *but I say a great intelligence of madness.*

Congolin's farm is an astonishment. To say it's a plot of land is to almost mischaracterize it. The farmland cotches on the flank of an extremely rocky karst limestone hill. I see projecting rocks standing erect in the earth like megaliths; upon closer inspection, however, they appear as what they truly are, under-sea rocks. I see the holes, notice the pathways that water has created, holes running to where one cannot see, sharp crevices and runnels in the white rock that gleams under the sun, dazzling the eyes. There are lots of them, everywhere, and the slope is extremely steep. Climbing up and through Congolin's cultivations, and looking behind me periodically at the steep drop below, I'm amazed at what he has done here. For many, this land would be considered uncultivable (Figure 1).

Figure 1. Lenford Smith, aka Congolin. Photo: Jason Allen-Paisant (February 2023)

I'm watching my step, anxious about pitching over the hillside all the way down into the wild tangle of lianas and untouched trees that conceal, perhaps, some chasm below me. I'm also trying to avoid stepping on the carrot shoots planted everywhere. Congolin walks with assured steps up and across the hillside, on land that to me seems precarious, even dangerous. Where I want to watch my step, move stealthily, gingerly, to avoid pitching backwards and onto the pointed rocks behind me, he seems to eat up the hillside, taking no visible care about where and how he positions his feet. The tiny spaces between the rocks brim with cultivation. There is yellow and negro yam, banana, plantain, papaya, okra, sugar beans, and all sorts of trees — avocado, pimento, castor, guinep, and more — on this flank of the hill. I'd not have been able to imagine so many things growing here because of the sheer smallness—what to *me* is smallness—of the cultivable space. But Congolin forces me to see this space differently, to adopt a different vision of scale. For Congolin, this land is not forbidding; it's what's available to him and what's his privilege to work with, to live with.

Around Jamaica, there must be loads of cultivation *grungs* like this, perched on rocky flanks, as if they could fall off, as if things could roll down the mountains, but their farmers cultivate them anyway. To engineer space is part of who we are as a people; and to cultivate an aesthetic out of the impossible is a necessity we have come to know over the centuries, as we've made life in this land, not just an in-bred instinct. Is there a kind of thrill in the capacity to do this? A part of the thrill may be the security Congolin gets from the tenure of this land, deemed unwanted, the security of knowing he won't be challenged for this space. This is land rejected by the plantation—there's something significant about this. Congolin's demeanour changes when he's in this space; it's his, he owns it.

Looking at Congolin's space and what he's made of it, I'm forced to think about Esiah Levy, a Black train driver turned farmer in the UK. Levy's relationship to the soil is one that astonished many in the years before his untimely death in 2019, and has been the subject of newspaper and magazine articles. He came to the attention of many because of his attempts at encouraging food growing amongst the young population in Britain, particularly among the demographics that have been most alienated from the land—that includes, of course, Black Britons, many of whose ancestors hail from the West Indies. Levy's parents were, themselves, Jamaican. But one of the main things that made this story of seeds and planting interesting is that Levy lived in the big city, London, and cultivated his crops on a very limited parcel of land, 'barely 15 by 9 feet', as Ruby Tandoh notes in her article 'Empire of Seeds'.[2] Her remark that Levy's small farm is 'packed with an astonishing 23 trees' sends my mind directly back to Congolin's land, in which Levy's determination to make the most of the land finds a striking parallel. Levy was showing just how much could be done with a tiny, backyard plot, just how much food could be grown—how much people could feed themselves in a self-sufficient manner, reducing their dependence on globalized food chains, in a country like England. And that proved attractive to many. So many people who felt alienated from the earth, from the foods they consume, and asked questions about globalized neoliberal economics and its effects on food, found in Levy's work something that was new and deeply inspiring. I can't help but think that what Levy was doing in 2017 and 2018 resembles what Congolin is practising silently on this Jamaican hillside, far away from the cameras of British media.

REFERENCES

[1] V.S. Naipaul, *The Enigma of Arrival* (London: Picador, 2002), p.93.
[2] Ruby Tandoh, 'Empire of Seeds. The Life and Dreams of Esiah Levy', *Medium*, 19 February, 2020, no page numbers.

CONTRIBUTORS

Keith Alcorn

Keith Alcorn is a Visiting Tutor in the Department of History at Royal Holloway, University of London where he teaches economic history. His research focuses on the introduction of exotic plants into Britain in the eighteenth and nineteenth centuries and the connections between British imperial expansion and plant introductions into Britain.

Jason Allen-Paisant

Jason Allen-Paisant is a writer and scholar. His creative writing encompasses poetry, memoir and critical life writing and addresses issues of time, race, class, and the environmental conditions underpinning Black identity. This interdisciplinary work explores embodied experience in the context of Afro-diasporic politics and world building. Jason is currently a Senior Lecturer in Critical Theory & Creative Writing in the Department of English, American Studies, and Creative Writing at the University of Manchester. Before this he was a lecturer in Caribbean Poetry and Decolonial Thought at Leeds University, with joint appointments in the School of English and the School of Languages, Cultures and Societies. He holds a Doctorate in Medieval and Modern Languages from the University of Oxford and joined the University of Leeds in 2016 as a Leverhulme Early Career Fellow. At Leeds, he served as board member of LUCAS (Leeds University Centre for African Studies) and was on the editorial board of *Callaloo: Journal of African Diaspora Arts and Letters.* His publications include *Thinking with Trees* (Manchester: Carcanet, 2021) and 'Reclaiming Time: On Blackness and Landscape' (*PN Review,* 47:3, 2021). In his forthcoming creative, non-fiction book, *Scanning the Bush* (London: Hutchinson Heinemann, 2024), Jason explores the ways of living with plants, herbs, trees and the earth, moving between his birthplace in Coffee Grove, Jamaica and Yorkshire, England, where he now lives.

Jeanne L. Gillespie

Jeanne L. Gillespie received a BA in Spanish from Purdue University and a Master of Latin American Studies from the University of Texas at Austin, concentrating on Art History and Anthropology. She completed her PhD in Spanish at Arizona State University and is Professor of Spanish and American Indian Studies at the University of Southern Mississippi. Recent scholarship examines the rhetoric and symbols of power in Indigenous narratives about the Aztec empire and the poetics of the *Cantares mexicanos.* Recent articles include 'Santos y guerreros: los relatos tlaxcaltecas de la conquista de Tenochtitlan' in *De conquistados a conquistadores. La raíz mesoamericana del virreinato de la Nueva España. Una nueva mirada*, edited by Alejandro Salafranca (2022) and 'Aztec Gardens: Representations of Political Power, Innovation, and Technology' with Nicolle Jordan in the *Southern Quarterly* Special Volume on Gardens and Gardening (2020).

Margaret Goehring

Margaret Goehring is a Professor of Art History at New Mexico State University (Las Cruces, NM) and is a specialist in late Medieval and Renaissance manuscript illumination and painting in France, the Netherlands and Belgium. She has published several articles on Franco-Flemish manuscript painting, and is also the author of the book, *Space, Place & Ornament: The Functions of Landscape in Medieval Manuscript Illumination* (2014) as well as co-editor of *Dressing the Part: Textiles as Propaganda in the Middle Ages* (2015). In addition to Medieval and Renaissance art, she also teaches American Folk & Outsider Art, the Art of China, and methodology.

Marlis Hinckley

Marlis Hinckley is a PhD candidate at Johns Hopkins University in the Department of the History of Science, where she studies plant and garden-related knowledge in the late Medieval and Early Modern period. Her focus is on the early modern Spanish empire, and she is currently writing her dissertation on the movement of plants between Spain and Mexico in the late sixteenth century. She held a Junior Fellowship at Dumbarton Oaks (2021-22) where she would like particularly to acknowledge Thaisa Way, Head of Garden and Landscape Studies. Marlis has also held a Fulbright-COMEXUS Research Fellowship (2022-23), among others.

Christine Lalumia

Christine Lalumia is an art, design and garden historian, with a particular focus on the period between late-nineteenth and mid-twentieth centuries. She is interested in the intersections between disciplines and in the interplay between the fine and decorative arts within a social history context. During her twenty one years as Deputy Director of the Geffrye Museum, London (now re-named the Museum of the Home), Christine worked on a range of projects, exhibitions and publications which explored the garden's role in domestic life and its centrality in constructing the idea of 'home', undertaking original research and writing extensively. She curated a number of seminal exhibitions, including *'A Garden within Doores'* which examined the long history of plants and flowers in the home. She was a co-curator of four separate but related exhibitions looking at the representation of the interior and the garden in Britain in paintings from 1670-2000, entitled *Home and Garden*. Since 2007, she has been a consultant lecturer on two separate MA programmes at Sotheby's Institute of Art, London, where she also co-edited two journals of occasional papers: *Creative Britain: Perspectives on twentieth century and contemporary design* (2012) and *Materials, methods and makers* (2014). Christine is also a long-standing Course Leader at the V&A, where she lectures regularly.

Michael Ann Mullen

Michael Ann Mullen is a garden historian. She has a BA in American History and MAs in Education from Columbia University, Visual Culture Theory from Middlesex University and Garden History from Birkbeck, University of London. She taught history in secondary school in the USA before coming to the UK where she worked as a freelance photographer for twenty years, then as an arts administrator at the London Arts Board and afterwards as a lecturer in History of Art at Middlesex University. She has been a co-convenor of the History of Gardens and Landscapes Seminar at the Institute of Historical Research since 2013. She was born and grew up in Detroit and returns there regularly.

Francesca Murray

Having worked in the design industry for the historic interiors brands of Cole and Son, Warner and Co and Zoffany for ten years, Francesca changed direction and studied horticulture and garden design at Berkshire Agriculture College, running her own garden design business for another ten years. Studying garden history at Birkbeck, University of London, in the evenings led to a Masters in Garden History at Buckingham University with a dissertation on the 'Orchids of the Rothschilds' (2015). After this she wrote *The Eighth Wonder of the World, Exbury Gardens and The Rothschilds* (Exbury Gardens Trust, 2019). She is in her third year of a PhD at Queen Mary, University of London, researching 'Nineteenth-century gardeners, nurserymen, and the associations that came to their aid'. She has published the following articles: 'The Stanwick Nectarine', *Garden History*, 50:2 (2022); 'The parochial nurserymen Youell and Sons', *Norfolk Gardens Trust Magazine*, No. 33 (Spring 2022); 'The Falstoff Raspberry', *Norfolk Gardens Trust Magazine*, No. 34 (Autumn 2022); 'An Absolute Passion: The Rothschilds' orchid collections at Gunnersbury Park, Tring Park, Exbury Gardens - and London's East End', *Rothschild Archive Review* (2013). She is a member of the Gardens Trust Education and Training Committee and of various county gardens trusts and is a regular speaker for the gardeners' charity *Perennial*, the name now given to the Gardeners' Royal Benevolent Society.

Katherine Myers

Katherine Myers taught garden history in adult education for many years, and has published articles on garden historical subjects in Britain and the United States.

Jesse O'Neill

Jesse O'Neill is a design historian and Senior Lecturer at the Chelsea College of Arts, University of the Arts London. His research in the design of built environments focuses on the modernizing lifestyles of former British colonies in Southeast Asia, which has addressed garden city planning, athletic swimming environments, industrial design promotions, and the architecture of colonial exhibitions. Jesse is a former Merewether Scholar (Australia) and Lee Kong Chian Fellow (Singapore), and has most recently published work in *Design and Modernity in Asia* (Bloomsbury), *BiblioAsia*, and *Chapters on Asia* (National Library of Singapore).

Pippa Potts

After a career writing and editing reports on Latin American economics and politics, Pippa Potts turned to garden history, obtaining an MA from Birkbeck College and a PhD from the Courtauld Institute of Art. She has been a convenor of the History of Gardens and Landscapes Seminar since 2018.

Alan Starr

Alan Starr obtained his DPhil at Sussex University on the subject of Wyndham Lewis, the novelist and painter. Most of his working life was spent as an IT consultant in the CIty. Recently he has had three books of local history published, as well as articles in publications by the Sussex Gardens Trust. He is currently an advisor to the Pevensey Mint House project.

SEMINAR CONVENORS

Dr Janet Waymark – founding convenor, 2003-2013

Michael Ann Mullen, Chair, 2013 – present

Christine Lalumia, 2013 – present

Stephen Smith, 2013 – 2021

Dr David Marsh, 2013 – 2021

Dr Pippa Potts, 2018 – present

Michael Gilson, 2021-2022

Dr Lyn Collier, 2020 – 2023

Stephen Radley, 2021 – 2023

Yvonne Hungerford, 2022 – present

SEMINAR THEMES, 2013 – PRESENT

2013/14

- Contemporary Representations of Gardens and Landscapes
- In the Shadow of War: British Gardens and Landscapes 1914-1945

2014/15

- The Garden and Science
- Exoticism in the 18th-Century British Garden

2015/16

- Changing Perceptions of the Landscape: What drives this – economics, politics, philosophy, aesthetics?
- Plant Introductions: Perspectives on their Importation and Survival

2016/17

- Gardeners and Gardening as a Profession
- Women in the Garden

2017/18

- Women in the Garden (continued from Spring 2017)
- The Context of the Reptonian Garden

2018/19

- Money, Money, Money (two terms)

2019/20

- New Perspectives on the Seventeenth-Century Garden (two terms)

2020/21

- Rus in Urbe: Greening Responses to Crises and Catastrophe, 1590s – present (two terms)

2021/2022

- Conversations across Continents: The Movement of Garden Ideas, Styles and Plants across the Globe (two terms)

2022/2023

- Gardens, Politics and Power (two terms)
- Roots and Routes: The Interdisciplinary Range of Garden History

Summer Terms

There are no specific programmes in the summer terms of each year. Instead those who are in the process of a research project, or have recently completed their work, are invited, via a call for papers, to give a presentation to the Seminar.

ACKNOWLEDGEMENTS

The list of contributors is evidence of the ever-widening pool of knowledge, research and interest in the history of gardens and designed landscapes that the Seminar has been able to draw on for its speakers. A debt of gratitude is owed to each and every one of them.

It is from their ranks that the contributors to this twentieth anniversary publication have been enlisted. For their willingness to participate in the project, to adapt their original papers or develop new ones, as well as putting themselves at the mercy of the editor, the convenors are profoundly grateful.

The project might never have happened if it had not been for the Birkbeck Garden History Group. Having already been most generous in providing the Seminar with financial support over the years, it was their suggestion that the convenors should consider publishing some of their contributors' work. Rising to the challenge, we have been very fortunate also to have tireless technical support from Susan Jellis and Joan Pateman. So for the spur and the support, thank you to the BGHG.

There has been invaluable support from other quarters too. One of the contributors, Katherine Myers, kindly agreed to take on the task of final proofreader. So thank you to her, and to the many people who gave support in the form of generous donations which have made it possible to cover costs.

Thanks are due too to the IHR for providing a place, both physical and virtual, where new post-graduate research could be aired and ideas exchanged.

Last but not least I would like to thank convenors past and present. It is a testament to their ideas and energy that the History of Gardens and Landscapes Seminar is celebrating its twentieth anniversary and now reaching a worldwide audience. My fellow members of the present cohort have also given a great deal of extra time and effort to this publication, which has been much appreciated.

Pippa Potts

Printed in Great Britain
by Amazon

27216885R00079